Contents

VOL 92   NO 3   AUTUMN

Poems

Essays

Reviews

The Questionnaire

Poet in the Gallery

Art

Poems

Anthony Caleshu

COLLABORATION: A DAY AT THE BEACH

The beach was emptying like an hourglass.

I saw an ex-lover who reminded me of an ex-lover.

It was late in the day and still her suit had not dried.

She pulled on her shorts over her suit.

Perhaps it was the way she bent that made me think of my ex-lover's body?

She once rolled herself around a beach ball, which was as kinky as we got.

Her friend said, *Just put a towel down under your suit. Don't worry about the interior.*

My current lover's feet were deep in the sand: coarse and grey.

I imagined how her beige shorts would darken when she sat in her wet suit.

Our table was way out on the pier, she said to her friend as she passed us.

The tide rolled in and a seagull squawked.

Like this? her friend asked her.

No, nothing like that, she said smiling.

I returned the smile and returned myself to burying my current lover in the sand.

Before the sun went down, she kissed me goodbye, letting me be the last one to leave.

STORMING THE BEACHES

Once with all the gusto of a twin-jet airplane
I attempted a late night harbour swim.

    I have seen the turbines of just such a plane
    suck in a man then spit him out without so much as a scratch.

I had to be rescued by a pretty lifeguard who later told me
about the prescription protection her dermatologist prescribed.

    I myself am always careful to unwind in the proper setting.
    When a submarine… cool your jets like a submarine.

Her golden hair was symptomatic of all of our war times.
Her golden tan was remarkable for there being no sun.

CHURCH FULL OF OBJECTIONS

In this church full of objections not one voice
can be heard over the nodding heads of today's couple.

    Into this woman's headpiece of turquoise feathers
    I am whispering everything unimaginable.

Because they too like the sound of God's well-wishes
they play dumb and illiterate, marking X in the air for I do.

    What if I told you that only yesterday she and I
    went through more positions than the hands of a clock?

For your silence now I'll tell you later how the lilies loomed,
making her sneeze and his eyes water.

Michael Henry

CHÂTEAU DE MONTFLAUX

The directions that you gave,
approaching through the *bocage*
past unsuspecting fields of corn

to where the road made a cedilla,
where it was waiting for me:
a *Sleeping Beauty* of a château

I wanted, like the handsome prince,
to raise from rank depredation.
The outbuildings, the *mutillés de guerre*,

I wanted to cast off their crutches.
The wrought-iron staircase with flights
of embroidery I wanted to book a waltz with.

The beautiful bull's-eye windows,
oeil de boeuf, like portholes from which
historical cannons keep watch.

The gatehouse where *Madame* is firing
her klaxon like a Parisian taxi-driver
and you check the beeps against the hour.

The directions that you gave,
approaching through the *bocage*
past unsuspecting fields of corn

to where the road makes a cedilla,
where you were waiting for me,
Beauty and the Beast, your back turned towards me –

a Caspar Friedrich *Rückenfigur.*

OHRWURM

If we could live our lives backwards
I'm sure they'd all be famous:
the Mexican film director with a black scarf
playing mad piano music in the Hofgarten café
and the shy Estonian violinist who has brought
her cellist boyfriend home to meet her parents.

The city has mulled wine on its breath
and a dusting of snow like salt on pretzels.
Far away snow is burning on the mountain.
I wrap myself in coat and scarf,
remember the sweet early morning smell of duvets
and my own first visit to Munich.

We drink blown-glass cups of *glühwein*,
help ourselves to pretzels from the wicker basket.
Candles are burning in our eyes.
It is turning dark, the city has
brazier breath, sweet chestnuts, *maroni*,
Punch and Judy stalls of *wurst* and *ochsensemmel*.

Outside the *Weinachtsliederkonzert*,
a woman is talking into her mobile phone:
Schön dass ich dich erreiche,
der Mercedes steht an der Ecke,
which I repeat over and over like a hit song.
The Germans have a word for it of course, *Ohrwurm*.

Jane Yeh

SEASIDE RESORTS

In Blackpool, I fainted dead on the spot.
The Illuminations were a gleam in the head donkey's eye,
Which eyed us suspiciously.

At Margate your ice-cream fell off its cone.
We settled for green-apple rock instead.

Between us something like Sussex lies – crab-shaped,
Humped in the middle, not quite symmetrical.
On the underside, tiny coves like mouths.

Boats landed at Hastings like tits coming home.
Their noses questioned me pointedly.

Combined, we would make an acceptable picnic spot,
Patchy in places. Birds on a branch, each a small container,
Containing bird-organs. And flocked.

On the end of Bournemouth pier, my boater flew into the Channel.
Luckily the candyfloss clung fast to its stick.

We are skirting England along its fringes, widdershins,
Like witches. A necklace circling a strange neck.
We outline the shape of it.

Torquay. The pebbles chattered under your feet.

Nicholas Laughlin

THREE POEMS

linger, "last", but last me, least
till steals this long-last longing 'long
to stolen sleep; such "lost" depends
(lost at whose lips?); lapsed, & left
its lustre, what was "left" (was love?
was "love"?): an age to find, a rusting
little rest from hunger: half
a hunger only: "half" itself
is hunger after whole, it holds
to have this all (as "all") unstalled:

halt is the whole of it, help of it, helving,
handy the hang of it, handing "past"
or "gone" or "one" to parsing, hung
at heel, & helter holding fast
till hails in a freak of the final fend of it
flight! from the fling to spring in falling,
free of fright in the frisk, the sting
of the worst-of-it's wending, fraught with that friending
flourish, the taste of hale, that thirst,
that thrust unfrail, that furl, that "first"

Fell from the sky, or I chose to fall,
blue-slate-shod & iron-shirted,
& all you knew was I came from a cloud,
a flying stone in a squall from the north.

The valley's breath was moist with the smell
of the months I passed – the sharp of green
or purple weeds crushed in the hand.
Weather exhaled me & I was glad

to lance the troubled air, surprised
the earth would have me so easy & fast.
Winds deserted me, my flight
was broken, elbows into grass.

You found me rising from the thick,
naked shoulders draped in clay.
I too was astonished, wished
I had a word to prove my way,

a better token than my haughty
bruises, forehead flecked with blood.
Your tender faces made me weep.
I would have trusted you the keep

of all the silences I learned
aloft. I wanted you to hear
the urge that tumbled me above.
I wanted you to take my love.

I will build you a new machine,
a more concise device to twist
& preen your elementary self.
I spied your scheme, I stole your blue-
print veins & ganglia, I solved
the cube root of your appetite
(that coefficient of desire),
the query pending from "and" & "and":

a wheel of small titanium hooks
(like question marks), pardelicate
with sinew springs, are measuring
the snag of your skin & sparkling
your nerves, as though a sort of spool
could catch trajectory & weave
a speed to thread you hot & keen
& clinging after rupted gleam:

the only architect, I loved
till I was raw & clean, a stone
to cut a piercer pulse, intent
to prang from you convulsed consent.

Peter Reading

In the tavern of Cristóval:
raucous music;
good people, their voices *ronco*;
cristal – goblet-glint of good wine,
glint-bright pane onto the Market Place,
lens of the eye,
lens of the eye.

And, in the tavern of Cristóval,
considerations that engender transient *coplas*.

In the tavern of Cristóval
consider the news of your new-dead mentor,
recall the fecund estuary,
the happy island –
field ornithology loses a limb
as today, here,
you re-read this sad, unwelcome epistle,
here, in the tavern of Cristóval.

        *

In this Market Place,
white eggs,
white lilies for the cadaver,
schmaltz watercolours depicting defunct rusticity,
atavistic tweed duds,
in this Market Place.

And, in this Market Place,
redundant kickshaws –
a busted butter-churn,
tarnished trash-trinkets,
gold, silver, brass, base metal,
cracked bourgeois crocks,
world's gear,

world's gear,
world's gear …
in this Market Place.

And, in this Market Place,
Stark Mortality,
offer you can't refuse,
in this Market Place.

                *

¿ That viejo,
dentro de Mesón Cristóval,
contiguo escaparate,
bebedor,   bebedor?,

¿ he has much tristeza, sí?,
¿ he has aflicción?,
¿ some troubles of dinero?

No, he is cansado,
viejo, simplemente.

                *

In the tavern of Cristóval,
those of us seeking the cure
(the maladies are divers –
do not name them, for we all know, we all know...)
assemble daily, daily to drain, to drain...

And from the window
of the tavern of Cristóval,
we view the comfy, complacent carpetbaggers
from the big tax-zones, early-retired,
fucking up the real estate
for the indigenous, impecunious honest.

And *outside* the tavern of Cristóval,
they think that it's O.K., that it's O.K.

*

In the tavern of Cristóval
many are there who have good lives;
many are there who have *tristeza*...

nevertheless,
in the tavern of Cristóval
all, all assemble daily.

John McAuliffe

ACTION

It is 3 a.m., on a wet night, and I'm stood
In the middle of a field,
Listening to *The Open Mind*, a repeat, on a walkman
When Corman with his wand and loudspeaker cone
Directs me, "Hey you", and then the long arm,
To walk across the field,
And to wade into the river
With the boom close to the water.
This is experience and I need experience.

Michael Hamburger

PLUM

Polymorphous from sloe
Through damson, bullace, pershore
To fleshy Victoria, exquisite gage,
If cousin to a canonical fruit.
Twelve times removed, it does not care:
Genealogy leaves it cold
As a freezer. But, philoprogenitive too,
Round or oval, it romps through colours,
Clouded dark-blue, purple to pink,
Goldenest yellow, green, variegations;
Puts out suckers all over the place
Yet will inbreed, interbreed,
The coarse with the highly cultured,
Unless grafted, restrained,
Dependent shamelessly
On its winged marriage brokers.

When the wingless claim reward
For the bother of ownership,
Selection, training, hygiene,
It hides from these predators,
In aerial loops evades
The picker bag wired to a stick,
Not ripe or caught till half-eaten,
Therefore discarded, disdained,
Escaping once more, to rot –
Down to the fertile stone
Which may raise again, anywhere,
Who knows what progeny, wilder;
And this, the random tree,
Once risen, may turn ascetic,
Thwart with mere leafage unnamed
The lust of curiosity.

Caroline Berrier

DADDY'S PUZZLES

In your letters to your Little Darling
Sent twice a week during
The long summer holidays,
You replaced the difficult words
With drawings of simple things.

Clever combinations of
Black cats, sailing boats
With perfect triangular sails,
Smiling suns and childish flowers,
Curly clouds above red roofs
Punctuated the news of your Paris exile.

Later, when we were not
On speaking terms,
After I learnt of your hidden past,
Perhaps you thought of sending me
Such a letter?

How would you have drawn
The difficult words? Milice:
Two men holding a third in a bath?
A makeshift tribunal in 1945:
Scary puppets waving a stick?
A ten years jail sentence:
A window cell with a bar for each year?
Or would it have defeated your ingenuity?

David Gravender

UHT-SANG

Dead slumber after three days driving
sullen midsummer interstates
Toronto to Bellingham; a makeshift bed
of sofa cushions, balled jacket for a pillow.
Too tired to be nervous, facing change
and a new horizon.
     Four a.m. A finger
of chill like the cold off bare iron
slipping beneath blanket and damp T-shirt;
my gut yawning sickly.
      Imperceptibly
through fogs of blood and skin, cotton-
mouthed, webby-headed, I begin
to waken: unsteady focus, gray light,
the room disjointed, unsettled.
       I can almost see
the spirits of the lost – slain or ignored – thought
to roam this hour of in-betweenness,
disturbing the dew on thorn and broom,
drawn always to one spot, one time,
ever anxious, unquiet. *What can I do,*
who will I be?
     Slowly light blooms outdoors, in,
prints the white carpet. The walls settle back,
the ceiling rises.
     A breeze, warm and damp, fragrant
with sea-salt, pine, and lilac,
breathes through the half-closed pane;
mind floating, my body lies limp, like one released,
who might begin to suspect himself
unfamiliar, possible,
     a presence
still waiting to be discovered, to be welcomed in:

as when, that June morning on Cape Spear,
dense Atlantic fog holding the sun at bay,
a fox, gaunt and ragged-brushed, ventured
from the tall, wind-beat scrub, so close
an outstretched hand could feel the warm
quick exhalation of his breath, before
he fled into the grass and mist,
                                        toward the cliffs
where we came suddenly, brought up short,
as wrapped in haze and silence, pink and yellow
in the sun now breaking though, an iceberg
real as spirit, fathomless, hovered offshore
and the day seemed at last itself, ready again
for beginning.

Susan Wheeler

GOOD GOODS

Having trafficked in ideas, they turned to birds, and soon depleted stocks in
quails, purple finches, black-capped chickadees, goldfinches, brown thrashers,
orioles. Surprise, at the fridge: Hilal, looking for her thimble. *A pity*. Then they
turned to cornerstones – to this and that, mainly to town halls; and despite their
efforts, supply engulfed demand. Marx hadn't helped. One hundred and sixty
billion was the usual ballpark on tie-ins for the pint-sized. They tried figurines,
energy shakes, cruises, whales and tulle. Brian yawned in the boardroom. The
girl Story: "If it fits, take six." Trumpet call – mouth cupped upon an ear – but
enslaved did they remain. Booted up to tacos at a drive-in. And they found
courtship a sudden object of the marketplace. Benjy: *This language sucks*. But
what to substitute? Lights, blinking, harbor at night, the boats lapped by sea –
even these they tried. Bill, in his lair, malt liquor. And so, coming down from the
agora, they wept from exhaustion and despair. And so, they filtered apparitions,
through dermatologist and butcher, and wept, despairing of return.

Keston Sutherland

ODE: WHAT YOU DO

What is death? It is the summation
statement of generations of prejudicial vote.
Dirt polishes up pretty good.

Extrude lust as a monofilament.
Provide in this sunken calibre its limpness,
memory, stick to – ice fries

spattering on, kicked-out then you braid
multiple small extruded, go
all tear-open like nobody's throat.

Point evacuate them, mean the sky
and snow-stars. Eros permits
this, Sabra and Shatila thread through

love they are a polyglactin of
areas unused in the lung.
The ring of fire shines and divorces.

Depressed the contrast switch, flew about you
which make? The autologous tissue snaps
replicates gel bollocks your head falls off.

Both sides of the vicryl too heal up point
the sky out. Its across-centre evocate at
snappy prolonged wind – this terrifying, and

correction no-one. I don't walk to the
bus stop, next I don't commit steel wish
they would shut up disgustingly break

up the tree, steel-features couldn't put it –
he hides and then buries his face. Burns
of evoked light too screech across the leg

cloud in that sky, polished beneath Seroxat,
across the leg that cloud. You manipulate
point defects in a flipper of liquid ash break.

Appropriate life is shredded in dreams
like soap in water. Dare to realize, and
weld forging of two, ask – get soapy

life mere twist into synecdoche, how you
stand for that. Into the position set
go there you go beautifully racing

flap of skin, hairdyer – the picking foam
set you go sadly beneath din stars
7.4% of the vote in London bang

nature into action potentials I don't see
how the alright. What a string of crap.
What a pang. To create, lather mix in

busted leg cloud not that. You dust
off the mimic, dust away my eyes.
An inner tradition of this exceeds panic.

Some cops boo. Evidently run about pin
airbag down make a ripped off picket
stunned. If you want to change the

tick alright. Everyone's so – lymphatic
drainage from a primary lust for, tends
to, agrees with, makes a stab at

wouldn't if you, swigs sickeningly that
drained call it a gab. Against the
lust to scrape you out set up objections

in a grid, circled with flowers. Some
them are gay. Imagine if you
did an orgasm every once you have to

accept at – sneezes away news, my
back is demotic, my front also is demotic,
leg is, penis is. I am not democratic.

Sing with the wind that bashes across asphalt
round her house with trees leaking
my bent eyes scattering salt over,

except that the – at first, I thought you
were crazy all that life, frittering
back happiness to offset

in the guise of compulsion, happiness itself.
You leg it. You cloud over.
Our government does not care about spitting

justice from the awash grin a shot
planned through the dark. What you do
in lights is a sort of shadow-preening

one tomorrow picket that it's used up
two soap polyglactin cloud cops
steel alright. If I can just that adapt.

Robert Saxton

THE STABLES

Where the stables stand
and the palace is destroyed,
there'll be haunting
by neither people nor horses.

History's placebo is porcelain,
the monkey orchestra and,
coarsely poignant
in their fragility, the roses.

Cryptic in this habitat,
one in a hundred might concede
molecular dust of ostlers,
soot-shadows of nurses.

Though my daughter borrows
silence effectively,
shuts herself away at midnight
with the sources,

soft blur of hands
is more than anyone expects
from so dreamless a place,
let alone faces.

THE DEVIL'S LIGHTHOUSE

First some advice for do-it-yourselfers – don't.
Stars are just pinpricks in the latrine tent.
All saints become themselves by accident.

The theatre's dark where torch-bearers have dried.
Upsticks your raindance to the streets instead.
Make shoppers chafe against their clamps of dread.

Tripping and fumbling couldn't matter less.
From damage, like a dolphin, arches grace.
The undetermined moth discovers lace.

THE FOUR WANTZ

The Four Wantz: vortex of dreams.
Braking, you breach the frontiers of the liminal.
As always on a roundabout –
    roundabouts are designed for no other purpose –
    collision with destiny is avoided.

Essex is more London than it seems.
Even in small towns hairdressers open late (not all).
They are confessionals, no doubt –
    to godfathers whose crimes are like those
    any family might have, embroidered.

Peter McDonald

SAN DOMENICO

My road from the bus-stop
takes me up twenty feet of steps
between high concrete walls
infested with scrubby dust and wasps,
graffiti, litter-falls,
and everywhere, from feet- to head-height,
gouged and scored, cut left and right
with bullet-holes

from fifty years ago
worn-in and weathered, that will stay so
for another fifty years,
where lizards scoot and insects go
forth, and back and forth
from shade to sun, while no one sees,
busy all afternoon for centuries
in the hot earth,

as I walk a few yards
down a line of stunned or basking cars
and the silent hospital,
then gates, and their stone eagle-guards
that look straight down the hill
as they take the longest of all long views
on walking men, just small enough to lose,
who hug the wall

as shelter from the sun
that burns straight down without reason
in the day's dead part,
and go home for the afternoon
to wait in shuttered light
half-reading books already half-read
with fruit and water and dry bread
and no appetite –

my destination too,
where I wait it out, as I have to,
with papers and ornaments
I can look over and look through,
a pile of cards unsent,
maps, glasses, and a handful of leaves
I cut this morning from three graves,
a kind of present

to myself, part souvenir
and part *memento mori*, laid out where
they wait to age and dry;
in the few hours till I appear
again on this last day
I open and close old books of lives,
smoothing their pages, to fill the first leaves
with leaves of bay.

Sam Sampson

THE EGYPTIAN PIANO CONCERTO

Boarding the keyboard diametrically
he anticipates the first step, before departure

at calculated intervals. Impressions skim
counter to boatmen in transit.
                            Nubian love songs

roll sleeves between progressions. I have seen the
moon chronologically ripen, in Hamilton, in Egypt;

a swallow's curvature, intersect the Nile, the Waikato.
What if this arrangement is flawed? After the finale

we will applaud. In time, retrospectively detach.

Philip Gross

STILLS

She cares for nothing but that caged
capuchin monkey, such a delicate
spoiled beauty that grabs slivers of fruit
peeled for it through the bars
then is fastidious.

*

He has let himself be delivered in a staff car,
with insignia. He feels only contempt
for those who commit such a breach
of etiquette in ignorance. Not him,
he has judged it time for such a move.

*

Oh, she is pale as a papery
Chinese screen. You're not the first to feel
you've seen through almost to the source diffused
that lights it from the other side. My advice?
Sling your hook, kid. Beat it.

*

His mother kept a hornbill with its beak
surgically removed, and fed it mashed nuts.
She kept a cock with no crow. Some say
her taste for such curiosities went further.
Those who know refuse to testify.

*

An imaginary monocle, thick
as the base of a whiskey glass,
screws the old magistrate's face in a wince
like a bad nut or the *agenbite*
of inwit. He was always half a frown.

*

She stares at the splash the young man made
in the deep end and has lost him
then is amazed by the broken shape of him,
greenish and shuddering, foraging sleekly,
halfway down the pool.

*

They say he is writing a treatise, the man
at the corner table. There might be a different café round him
that none of us sees. His words fall into place like locusts
settling their wings. The armies that will march
are polishing their boots but do not yet know why.

*

The bell clanged of its own will.
Farm dogs, mongrels, lapdogs from the basket
gathered in packs. Now, the church dome
hangs ruptured by earthquake, now
the sky's own fresco showing through.

*

The girl, one of the implacably-
smiling waiters' children, daps a ball
in the bin yard, hour after hour, kicking a bare leg
up and over, muttering a counting game.
If we could catch the language, then we'd know.

*

There will be a dance
tonight, they whisper,
lit by snow light
only, that
and a border-guard's moon.

Simon Coppock

LOVE POEM

You are roses to me.

Not like, but are

　　　　nor are roses

　　　but

　　　　　　roses.

But you are roses to me.

Medbh McGuckian

MY CARMELITE FAMILY

It had taken me more than an hour
To come to life, under the rose-encrusted
Influence of the star-driven morning.

A blue a bit too pastel, with all its accessories,
A colour he could not have given us
In a hundred years, familiar but shallow,

Intense but guarded, multiplied the sensations
Of his different flesh, though not
My ability to return the increased gaze.

Breathtakingly tactile, his beautiful
Carnal mask distanced the white reserve
Of the paper, yet brought it closer

To his cornerstones, the perfect control
Of his hands' immense fresco about to move.
This eye reddened at his blood-red

Accents and the pure indication
Of his heart belonging low that owned
Casts of my arms and feet.

So that the way we sat was a hearth
From which the layers emanated,
Walking into the seacoil of a song.

HOLY SATURDAY JUDAS

A stage-set tree whose tapering force
Chokes off the night sky's looped apart
Curtains, embracing nothing, gathering
Nothing in, she appears to be neither
Wooden nor stationary, her body cramped
Forward with the knees into the chest.

No sign of her shoulders marking out
Points, flaky-robed in a robe of wings,
A small boat supports the heavy red
Of her foot, while the fingers of either hand
Are a flared, upward-turning bell,
Colliding with the off-shore evening air.

A forest she is, in simple movement,
An old-growth forest surrounded
By autumn's shell in the pale-warm spring
Zest of the hours, whose single arm
Dreaming with pressed and netted hair,
Undercuts its treeness.

The faraway, nearby, translake
Mountain, cruel where the black
Passes over, tender in its silver-toned
Puckerings of preparation,
Has all the time in the world
For its long, slow looking.

She has worked that voice like copper
Along the slender, swooping rib
Of a well-chosen feather, to the most ethereal
Mouth-end of the mock skull,
Where a dry sea, an ovoid blue,
Opens like an unfleshed being.

And the stray, deersigned messages
Within her once-velvet throat,
Lower the mask that earth's skin
Has given her, into the birdcage
Of the muses, into its triple visage,
As if she asked to be shelved that way.

Robert Crawford

FROM THE TOP

for Iain Galbraith

From the top, breathless, feet in the clouds,
I see how at the ankle-high horizon

Dutch fields are Berber rugs in a bazaar;
Red tiled roofs pave the village far below;

I clock the non-stop Colorado River,
Dandelion heads unblown in East Westphalia,

Bings, sunlit mesas of the Scottish Lowlands,
Stretching towards nettled woods whose watermills'

Dust harps, thick burr stones, and dark gravelocks
Promise half firlots or a grinding halt.

I spot South Island beckoning Amazonia
Past Arrochar and Wiesbaden, I watch

Shackleton's shadow cross the Southern Lights
And swallows brushing Arabic on air,

That canny man of 78 who built
The biggest sugar mills in Puerto Rico,

Horn spoons, a rotting, gnawed-at Hong Kong torso,
And Carrick Castle inlaid on Loch Goil,

All things improbable, as God's my witness,
Bamiyan Buddhas, Easter Island heads,

And everything I see here from the top
Is overlooked by bens and glens of stars.

Chris Emery

SPIDERS

the monsters are entering the church
smiling & twisting our children
that priest pours tv pots
on trays of tiny spiders

& we are washing each utensil
licking the suture of the future
in an elemental sink
over there the wrecks are stuck

in the family of petrol waters
over here we are kissing
in the factory trough mending numbers
making some suggestion

about these lungs & spiritual
fittings / the indolent bolts
on the eyelids of our children
it should maim the vacuum at least

but that is a smallish truth perhaps
& so with the holes of our bones
shrieking with crows or poised
lascivious on the sweaty peculiar legs

of that priest / the phosphorus
mouth all filthy talk again
on the majesty of one single gas
& worried meat still singing lost

squatting down on kid juice
just like that we stare straight
through to family fingers working
in the tight beautician's clinic

true / or else it is us ruining
the old pneumatic country
awkward birds still loose beyond
this evening's wires & membranes

so listen because we got this for you
with stinking crutches
yanking on children
for years to come

we can strain all dog thought
to fathom out those flying feet
(we saw them once stabbed in the fridge)
& putting necessary pain in mind

just yesterday you ruined ten
but now their solid dresses fritter
as we play tig in the yard
beside the old distillery drum

so think of this before you go
into the metal tirade of dead plants
with all your children sinking
in the knuckles of the truth

Fergus Allen

LIKE MINDS

Of course you have no interest
In the condition of my fur-lined soul,
Nor I in that of yours.

Solids of revolution,
Artefacts without fingerprints or scratches
Might satisfy us both

But are in short supply.
The marks of aliens are all around us,
Attention-seeking curlicues,

Jewellery mixed with mucus,
An unwillingness to produce straight lines
When straight lines have been suggested

Or a determination
To draw lines straight against the best advice.
The hunger and treading down –

And the animus behind it!
But do you and I really care for feelingless
If perfect crystal spheres,

Whose lugubrious music
Is only wind keening around the dormers
As a low edges eastwards,

Impersonal as physics?
It's belonging to the cohort that matters,
Everyone else go hang.

And the delicious glue
That holds what were the boys and girls together
Is coded in Linear A,

Opaque to exegesis
As the diary of an iguanadon
To a mammalian reader.

Not that I look for empathy.
As I hinted, my soul is warm and snug,
Watching Petrushka's drama

In my private viewing room,
Though my tears form more slowly than they used to.
Maybe our tastes diverge,

But have I your attention?
Should I knock on the plasterboard and ask
Is anybody there?

This place is full of furniture
That I never have need of, and the skylight
Is useless to man or beast.

Simon Smith

UPSIDE-DOWN SONG

Coloured round objects appear first
Separated out in numbered sections.
Start with the life and get back to me.
Cloud burst to step in
Walk out to. Twelve minutes later the lot
Stair rods air water buckets loads of garden fence washing-line
Then here comes the shed whatever you like really neither
One side nor the other drops
Floats a bit of a stir neither to the side
I prefer things that float writers writing
Popped back into shape
The air steady but the other
Way round left-handed don't you know I don't
Count you way up too
Late the field opens out green
Below blue dropped out of the slow
Movement dewy web you make what you
Make is what pearly silk of a grey room as egg
White to white grubs.

PULL

It's soon my home the echo
Kind of hop forward
Blinds down
Ask the relevant question about now
The eye a bookmark a note black
Arrow kinda if an idea were
A light-bulb better than the album well
We could but we won't
Start all over again
You got me here in the first place
Return plop

NOW WHAT

It sounds it
Thoughtless
Easy easy
Takes you to that bridge
Calls up the signs to keep
Things going we could well
You could x-ray
The title towards me
Bounce then plop
Plonk that's right

HEAPS

You walked sing-song to the shape not who
You think it is though
A closing movement in the way of looking
Budge in the other direction makes a note make
A note tipped with your sour kiss as collusion
As collision leaves a signature dissolved to
The next disclosure that's settled then
All traffic stopped next
To the ticket kiosk except blue cars the rest drive on
Air steady film a kind of flame flies through
The coffee table to form thought
A letter I'm writing to someone else. Or this
You wouldn't know. End with a little biog
Or a hard-boiled egg.

Essays

DAVID HERD

Enthusiasm

THERE IS A brief, beautiful Frank O'Hara poem called "Radio". Here it is in full:

RADIO

Why do you play such dreary music
on Saturday afternoon, when tired
mortally tired I long for a little
reminder of immortal energy?
                                        All
week long while I trudge fatiguingly
from desk to desk in the museum
you spill your miracles of Grieg
and Honegger on shut-ins.
                                        Am I not
shut in too, and after a week
of work don't I deserve Prokofieff?

Well, I have my beautiful de Kooning
to aspire to. I think it has an orange
bed in it, more than the ear can hold.

Did you enjoy that? My guess is that you will have. It would have been wrong to call it beautiful otherwise. So supposing you did enjoy it, what do you do with it?

You could read it again, of course, linger over it, grow more accustomed to its supple irregular rhythms, to its confident shape, its unembarrassed tone. You could copy it out, into a notebook or onto a card-file, not for any obvious reason perhaps, except some barely defensible instinct to preserve. (As if the poem was so good there just should be more copies of it, in case all the other copies in the world should happen to be destroyed.) You could analyse it, get to know its workings better, observing, for instance, the play of the poem's address, between the directness it adopts towards the radio itself and its indirect-ness (albeit open) towards the reader. You could notice the cleanness of its phrasing, the way its five short sentences make use of and disregard line-endings in equal measure. You might even make something of this happily informal poem's gesture towards chiasmus, the near mirroring of "tired" and "tired", of "mortal" and "immortally", of "museum" and "spill" – "spill" is a great word – of "shut-ins" and "shut-in", of "week" and "work", of "de Kooning" and "aspire to". Alternatively, you could present the poem to somebody else, hand it on because you think they might like it.

This is what the poem does. Tired after a week of work – and I will come back to work; flanêur that he was, Frank O'Hara was a great poet of work – O'Hara implores his radio for sustenance, for music that will pick him up and keep him going: Grieg, Honegger, Prokofieff. At the same time, of course, because he too is being listened to, he hands these composers on. Grieg and Prokofieff were well enough known in the 1950s. Honegger wasn't. O'Hara, however, has no reason to suppose the reader won't find Honegger as sustaining as he does. Nor does the reader. Honegger is handed on. Which is ok, of course, with composers, in that because the radio spills them (weekdays anyway) all O'Hara has to do is mention their names. The reader can do the rest. The de Kooning is more difficult, which is why O'Hara takes a moment to describe it. Except that as soon as he starts to, he realises he can't. It's too beautiful, exceeds description: "more than the ear can hold".

The de Kooning with a bed in it was a gift from a painter. O'Hara received many such gifts – from friends, collaborators, artists whose work he had advocated (both as an occasional art reviewer and as an exhibitions organizer at the Museum of Modern Art). When he died, however, in 1966, killed in a motor accident on Fire Island, and as Russell Ferguson tells us in *In Memory of My Feelings: Frank O'Hara and American Art*, O'Hara owned very few of these canvases. Sometimes, no doubt, he had mislaid them – as he would frequently mislay his poems (moving onto the next before he had filed the last, more interested in the action than the product). More often than not, however, he would re-present the canvases: to other collaborators, other friends. Faced with what you might call the enthusiast's question, *What do you do with what you like?*, and appreciating all the implications of acquiring culture, Frank O'Hara passed it on.

> Enthusiasm: "the intensiveness and vigour of ... sensations ... which as it were hurries the mind out of itself; and which is vented in warm and vehement description, exciting in every susceptible breast the same emotions that were felt by the AUTHOR himself". (William Duff, 1767)

Passing it on is only one thing you might do with something you like. Another thing to do would be to hold on it. This impulse is understandable, and is also, in a narrower sense, an enthusiast's, the enthusiast in question being the collector. And of course to some degree or other most poets are collectors, the major ones anyway, there being obvious affinities between the two habits of mind: the discriminations, the obsession with detail, the subtle variations within a form. Wallace Stevens, for instance, collected *objets d'art*, commissioning all his friends who went to Europe – the Stevens themselves always holidayed at Key West – to bring him back something beautiful. William Carlos Williams, on the other hand, who holidayed in Paris, collected chicken wire and farm implements. Marianne Moore collected animals. As did Elizabeth Bishop. Although Bishop, being a post-war poet, had a tendency to lose things. W. H. Auden collected readers. John Ashbery collects everything. Then loses everything. Then collects it again. Then, of course, there's T. S. Eliot.

From the point of view of enthusiasm, as from most points of view, T. S. Eliot is a vexed case. So, in theory at least, or at least according to "Tradition and the Individual Talent", poetry is all about passing things on, or rather, as Eliot prefers to describe it, "handing things down". (Elsewhere, of course, he says that the things "handed down" must also be "stolen". But this is to get ahead of the argument.) The poet, then, according to Eliot's essay, is nothing more, or rather nothing less, than the medium through which the virtues of poetry pass. Or as Eliot puts it, "What happens is a continuous surrender of himself as he is at the moment to something which is more valuable. The progress of an artist is a continual self-sacrifice, a continual extinction of personality." Viewed in terms of "enthusiasm" this is very promising, if, let's be frank, a touch melodramatic. What Eliot is describing is, after all (the aura and incense aside for a moment) the passing on of that which you find beautiful. And yet Eliot makes no mention of enthusiasm. Should he? Well, put it this way, he struggles not to, and certainly he would have known that he wasn't doing so. Because certainly he would have known that enthusiasm, as it derives from the Greek, means the taking in or being possessed by a god; that it was all about the awful daring of a moment of surrender; that, stripped of its religious content, it means giving voice to something more than oneself: the tradition of European literature for instance. And certainly he would have known, also, that from, say, Plato to Emerson, major commentators on poetry had understood the poetic act precisely as enthusiasm: as the moment of surrender by which it becomes possible to voice things greater or more important than oneself. Curious, then, that in his essay on tradition and the act of surrendering to tradition, Eliot should not mention a tradition of self-surrendering so intimately connected with poetry.

But not that curious. Scroll forward a few years, and what Eliot actually surrenders himself to is the Church of England. And there is nothing, of course, which the Church of England suspects more than an enthusiast: than all those Adamites, Anabaptists, Antinomians, Brownists, Familists, Independents, Quakers, Ranters and Socinians. All those Christians, in other words, who, in the seventeenth and eighteenth centuries, wanted to get more intimate with their God than Anglican structures would allow, and many of whom went to America to try and do so.

"Tradition and the Individual Talent" is the essay of a man trying not to be an enthusiast. *The Waste Land* is not, in the generous sense of the term, an enthusiast's poem. Reading it is like walking around one of those private collections – The Wallace in London, for instance, or in Boston the Isabella Stewart Gardener – in which you are allowed to see everything, but in which nothing is quite made public, in which all the items are stamped with the collector's mark.

To put it another way: a reference in a Frank O'Hara poem is always to a book you really would enjoy reading. An allusion in T.S. Eliot is to something you ought already to have read. "My heart is in my / pocket, it is Poems by Pierre Reverdy". "Cf. the Dirge in Webster's *White Devil*."

> Enthusiasm: "a living fire which feeds by degrees, which feeds by its own flames and whim, and far from becoming feebler as it expands acquires new strength in proportion to the extent that it spreads and communicates". (Diderot, 1751)

Of the many things to which Frank O'Hara surrendered himself, by no means the least important was lunch. This was a big decision. Lunch, of course, is always a big decision: when to have it, whom to have it with, whether or not to have the corn-beef hash. What I mean, though, and over and above these always pressing questions, is that Frank O'Hara's decision to write poems through lunch (he published his *Lunch Poems* in 1964) was a big decision in terms of American poetry.

American poets have for a long time given serious thought to matters of diet. In his essays on "The Poet" and on "Inspiration" Emerson discourses at length on all manner of appealing intoxicants: wine, mead, narcotics, coffee, tea, opium, the fumes of sandalwood. In the end, though, and citing Milton as his authority, he urges the poet to drink "water out of a wooden bowl". "The poet's habit of living should be set on a key so low and plain, that the common influences should delight him. His cheerfulness should be the gift of sunlight;

the air should suffice for his inspiration, and he should be tipsy with water." Poetry, Emerson insists, is not "Devil's Wine", and the true poet, he urges, and he is very earnest about this, will be at pains to avoid French Coffee. (American coffee, being on the whole weaker, is possibly acceptable. Emerson doesn't say.) Likewise William Carlos Williams, who all his life argued with Pound that the poet should eat bread. Which is perhaps not to say that he or she shouldn't eat plums, but that in general, as for Emerson, Williams thought the poet should be susceptible to the common influence. Pound, on the other hand, argued that the poet should eat caviar. "Civilization becomes admirable when people begin to prefer a little of the best to a great deal of the pasty" (*Guide to Kulchur*). Prufrock, it should be remembered – how could one forget? – procrastinates in the face of a peach.

There are two questions here. Emerson's is quite literal. What, he is asking, is the best fuel for poetry? This is what Emerson was always asking, American poetry being in a sorry state at the time. Always the question driving his criticism was not what book to say yes to or what book to say no to, but how best to inspire great poems; how to enthuse; how to make poetry happen. All aspects of the poet's intake are therefore important to him: his environment, his reading, whether or not he drinks wine. The Williams-Pound question is rather different, being about how, and in what company, the poet should conduct themself, about what kind of materials the poet should let into his or her poem. Scratch an American poet and often as not, as with Williams, they come up a Puritan. Ezra Pound was a Puritan-Aristocrat.

O'Hara, though happy enough with a cheeseburger, was probably closest, among American poets, to Wallace Stevens when it came to diet; to the breakfast Stevens's woman has that "Sunday Morning", to the "Complacencies of the peignoir, and late / Coffee and oranges in a sunny chair". But the issue with O'Hara is not so much what he ate – if push came to shove he would probably have eaten anything – but with how food figured in the poetic process. By writing poems through and about his lunch, by taking the question of fuel inside the poem, O'Hara made inspiration, the things that keep the poet going, and the things that keep other people going, the explicit stuff of poetry. The poet is a person through whom things pass. Poetry is a medium – and here Eliot's term is helpful, although somehow when he uses it one thinks of Madame Blavatsky – for passing on that which makes the poet enthusiastic: Prokofieff, instant coffee, Lana Turner, Boris Pasternak, chocolate malted, Rachmaninoff, Mary Desti's ass. O'Hara's poems keep people and poetry going.

The older O'Hara got the longer the lunches. So on 30 August, 1961, he sat down for "Déjeuner Bill Berkson". The meal is commemorated in his late poem "Biotherm" ("Biotherm" being one very extended lunch):

> Hors-d'oeuvre abstrait-expressionistes, américain-styles, bord-durs, etc.
> Soupe Samedie Soir à la Strawberry-Blonde
> Poisson Pas de Dix au style Patricia
> Histoire de contrefilet, sauce Angelicus Fobb
> La réunion des fins de thon à la boue
> Chapon ouvert brûlé à l'Hoban, sauce Fidelio Fobb
> Poèmes 1960–61 en salade
>
> > Fromage de la tour Dimanche 17 septembre
> > Fruits des Jardins shakspériens

Biscuits de l'*Inspiration* de Clarence Brown

Vin blanc supérieur de Bunkie Hearst
Vinc rouge mélancholique de Boule de neige
Champagne d'*Art News* éditeur diapré
Café ivesianien "Plongez au fond du lac glacé"

Vodka-campari et TV

O'Hara, like Stevens, got his appetite from the French, who have eaten well ever since Rabelais, ever since Pantagruel filled himself up on *grands pastés*:

de venaison,
d'allouettes,
de lirons,
de stamboucqs,
de chevreuilz,
de pigeons,
de chamoys,
de chappons,
pastés de lardons,
pieds de porc au sou,
croustes de pastés fricassés,
corbeaux de chappons,
fromaiges,
peches de Corbeil,
artichaulx …
caviat

Pantagruel, like Gargantua, is Rabelais's enthusiastic figure for writing – that through which everything is passed. Like Rabelais, O'Hara understood that food belonged inside the poem: enthusiasm sustaining communication.

Enthusiasm: "Yet, from an aesthetic point of view, enthusiasm is sublime, because it is an effort of one's powers called forth by ideas which give to the mind an impetus of far stronger and more enduring efficacy than the stimulus forwarded by sensible representations." (Kant, 1790)

Not all poets should be gargantuan of course. There is more than one way to eat a lobster. There are pressing reasons, however, and reasons beyond aesthetics, why poets should make it their business to enthuse. Chief among these reasons, as O'Hara's "Radio" implies is work. Or rather as it features in contemporary British society: WORK.

Frank O'Hara worked hard. He was good at and very committed to his job at the Museum of Modern Art. He also worked tirelessly on behalf of writers, artists, and musicians he admired: advising them, exhorting them, circulating their work. It is a wonder he ever found time to write any poems, and is integral to his achievement that he did. Huh? What I mean to say is, O'Hara's achievement lay not least in developing the discipline and the aptitude to write whenever he wasn't working. Delighted not to be working, O'Hara's poems invariably tell us he isn't – it's the weekend, its lunch-time, he's on the train, he's in Paris. Wherever and whenever, he isn't working.

And as often as not, because he isn't working, O'Hara becomes gargantuan, in a strictly positive sense, in the Rabelaisian sense, a multiple and various self. Or, as "In Memory of My Feelings" memorably has it:

> I am a Hittite in love with a horse. I don't know what blood's
> in me I feel like an African prince I am a girl walking downstairs
> in a red pleated dress with heels I am a champion taking a fall
> I am a jockey with a sprained ass-hole I am the light mist
> > in which a face appears
> and it is another face of blonde I am a baboon eating a banana
> I am a dictator looking at his wife I am a doctor eating a child
> and the child's mother smiling I am a Chinaman climbing a mountain
> I am child smelling his father's underwear I am an Indian
> sleeping on a scalp
> > and my pony is stamping on the birches,
> and I've just caught sight of the *Niña*, the *Pinta* and the *Santa Maria.*
> > What land is this, so free?

Supposing something, or somebody, is being passed on here, the obvious thought is that it is Whitman: "I am large, I contain multitudes". And Whitman himself of course was a great poet of work, "Song of Myself", like "Song of Occupations", taking time out to honour, among others, America's professions and trades: "farmer, mechanic, artist, gentleman, sailor, quaker, prisoner, fancy-man, rowdy, lawyer, physician, priest". You're doing a fine job there boys. Keep it up.

Except that O'Hara doesn't honour work and workers – there are construction workers in silver hats, of course, but that's another essay. What O'Hara does with work, instead, is exceed it. Whitman was excessive also, but in his expansiveness, he was always re-enshrining the American division of labour. As good, he contends, to be a prostitute as a president. Which is not true of course. What's good is not to work, not to be constrained by work, not to be instrumental, not to fill in forms; not to apply for funding, not to process applications, not to account for oneself, not to be defined. O'Hara knew this, and so in his pluralistic moments, he sounds not so much like Whitman as a surreal version (and I mean a *surreal* version) of those much more knowing nineteenth-century poets of the division of labour, Marx and Engels. Not, of course, that O'Hara read Marx. Marx, however, read a lot of poetry:

> Possible for me to do one thing today and another tomorrow, to hunt in the morning,
> fish in the afternoon, rear cattle in the evening, criticize after dinner, just as I have a
> mind, without ever becoming hunter, fisherman, herdsman, or critic.

Do you work too hard? Does you work spill into everything? Are you barely distinguishable from your job? O'Hara's enthusiasm, his gargantuan appetite for life, is a reminder, always, that people are capable of more.

Enthusiasm: "a true and real possession of some extrinsical superior power … producing [such] effects and operations … as speaking strange languages, a temporary learning and the like". (Meric Casaubon, 1655)

The paradox, of course, is that becoming an enthusiast, in the sense, at any rate, that is being described here – becoming a person who passes art on, reminding one's contemporaries what they are capable of – is extremely hard work. And not least because always enthusiasm is in danger of spinning off into mentalities and practices less than itself: egotism, fanaticism, mania, obsession, eccentricity, boosterism. Take Damien Hirst.

Damien Hirst is a serious artist. Serious in the way that Frank O'Hara thought his contemporaries in American sculpture, David Smith and Reuben Nakian, were serious. Writing about these sculptors in *Kulchur* magazine, and taking the opportunity to urge the Lincoln Center to be more generous in its selection of exhibits, O'Hara asserted that:

> Modern American sculpture is presently at a very great height of development … Most … as in the case of Smith and Nakian, either have executed, or projected, work of a scale and grandeur which cannot at present be accommodated in either our public or private situations for one reason or another … Lincoln Center is one of the few foreseeable possibilities to rectify this situation and, in so doing, allow our sculptors to make real their dreams, dreams which follow so closely Keats' great aspiration: "I am ambitious of doing the world some good".

Hirst, it seems to me, is also, in part, ambitious of doing the world some good. And he understands, just as O'Hara knew that Smith and Nakian understood, that if art is to do good, then being art, as a basic requirement it must excite. O'Hara, whose threshold for boredom was refreshingly low, once contended, by way of merry provocation, that among American poets only Whitman, Crane, and Williams were better than the movies. Hirst's provocation begins with his titles: "And now my pretty One, I feel I need your undivided attention", "He Tried to Internalize Everything", "The Physical Impossibility of Death in the Mind of Someone Living", "I want to Spend the Rest of My Life Everywhere, With Everyone, One to One, Always, Forever, Now". Only an artist who assumes it as his duty to reach beyond himself, to "play" on a very large scale, to become more, in his work at least, than his society would have him, would come up with titles as capacious as these. Or with "Hymn", Hirst's twenty-foot man. Extravagantly humanistic in its physical display – the man in question has his innards exposed – "Hymn" is painted in a bronze paint that will, in time, decay. It is thus of a piece with much of Hirst's other work, tracking the processes by which things pass through a body, and through which a body itself must pass. Which is not a new theme obviously – what Hirst is commenting on is death – but it is in the oldness of this theme that Hirst's enthusiasm consists. Which is to paraphrase Eliot, for whom one error in poetry was "to seek for new human emotions to express; and in this search for novelty in the wrong place it discovers the perverse". At his best Damien Hirst expresses old emotions: love, wonder, frustration, rage. And the excitement of his work consists not simply in his decision to take British art by the scruff of the neck, in his insistence that the sun shines today also, but in his decision to make of himself and his work that through which the emotions of art would pass.

The problem is, and the artist is not solely to blame for this, the grand emotions are not all that pass through Hirst's work:

> Selling the big guy [Hymn] for a million pounds. I mean Jay [Jopling] said to me the other day, "Aren't you worried about Charles putting it in the Saatchi Gallery before it goes to New York?" I said, "A million pounds, Jay. A million pounds". I'd sell my fucking granny for a million pounds … A lot of what I say is hypocritical, but I think with a benchmark of a million pounds you owe it to everyone around you and behind you to take the money.

And good luck to him, and to all his ventures – I have heard his restaurant did a very good lunch. There is a problem, however, in the fact that in making art Hirst has so readily made money, Saatchi's money to be precise: because Saatchi is one of those collectors who takes art out of circulation; because when enthusiasm meets money some kind of distortion invariably results. Appetite is a highly desirable quality in an artist. The problem arises when the artist inflates.

A better example is a career with quieter beginnings. In 1850, at the age of thirty, having only journalism and some unpublishable short-stories to his name, Walt Whitman decided to become a poet. Or rather, he decided that America needed a poet, and that in the absence of any other obvious candidates it would have to be him. Five years later, and without showing anything to anybody in the meantime, Whitman published *Leaves of Grass*.

Whitman's process of re-invention is documented in his notebooks: he was forever writing advice to himself; urging himself to sufficient ambition: trying out various modes of address. But what is also documented there is his extensive programme of reading: Whitman, who hitherto was not especially well read, undertaking, in the process of becoming a poet, to read the great works of world literature he understood it as his business, as a poet, to make new. (Melville did this also, though he went further than Whitman, publishing his notebooks at the beginning of *Moby-Dick*. Those quotations which perplexingly begin the novel – from *The Bible*, from Montaigne, from Rabelais, from Spenser, from Shakespeare, from Milton, from Jefferson, from Hawthorne – being a list of the books Melville thought it necessary to read if one was to write, or enjoy, the next great book.) Whitman had advantages of course: no writing group, no coterie, no grants to apply for, no prizes, no cliques. Just Emerson urging him to do something marvelous. And a willingness, when necessary, to make a spectacle of himself.

When he was young, trying to become a poet, Whitman would ride the trolley buses in New York, declaiming Shakespeare, steeling himself maybe, for all the extraordinary utterances he had yet to voice. Imagine it, though; how embarrasing. You get on a bus, some guy starts quoting Shakespeare. Spilling words. Where do you put yourself?

Enthusiasm: "No enthusiasm is permitted, except at the opera".
(Ralph Waldo Emerson, *English Traits*)

Total Immersion

LINDA A. KINNAHAN

DENISE RILEY'S POETRY delights in the play of language, but it is deadly serious play. The social nature of poetry assumed and promoted by her work complements and draws upon the social engagement of her life as a theorist, teacher, activist, and poet. Riley's work in all of these areas often circles around the category of "woman", asking difficult questions not just about the "woman poet" but about notions of womanhood in the contemporary Western world.

While known internationally as a theorist (she is the author of *War in the Nursery: Theories of the child and mother, Am I That Name? Feminism and the category of "Women" in history*, and editor of *Poets on Writing: Britain 1970-1991*, among other works), and despite her important presence within discussions of poetics, Riley's work as a poet has not been as widely recognized as it should be, for a number of reasons. One would be her endorsement of an experimental poetics; a second, and related reason would be her choice to publish with small presses. A third reason has to do with gender and the relatively minimal recognition granted British women poets within a male-dominated poetry scene over the past twenty-five or thirty years. Certainly, the Women's Movement of the seventies, and subsequent forms of feminist theory and literary criticism, have brought the literary accomplishments of women into fuller view. However, the aesthetics of accessibility and reportage have most often been valued in promoting contemporary women's – and especially feminist – poetry. Riley's experimental and intellectualised poetics does not sit easily with the dictate to "tell one's story", as valuable as that initiative is, for her work questions whether fully knowing and shaping one's own experience, free of cultural and linguistic mediations is ever possible.

Born in 1948 in Carlisle and adopted by a working class couple, who raised her in Gloucester, Riley was an early convert to feminist ideas, honed through teenage readings of de Beauvoir and Woolf, until, in the late '60s she joined the Abortion Law Reform Association and entered the Women's Liberation Movement, also taking part in demonstrations against the war in Vietnam. Riley's involvement with feminist activism in the '70s brought her into contact with thinking of the political left. Studying Moral Sciences and Fine Arts at Cambridge during these years, she went on to receive a D.Phil in Philosophy at Sussex University.

As a poet, Riley has been closely associated with the "alternative" poetry scene in England. Her friendships with poets in Cambridge, particularly Wendy Mulford, prompted her to publish her first collection, *Marxism for Infants* (1977) with Mulford's small press, Reality Street. A network of British poets looking beyond Britain, including Mulford, J. H. Prynne, John James and others, and the "large and ambitiously international" Cambridge poetry Festivals, gave Riley access to the work of poets outside of Britain, including Americans like John Ashbery, Frank O'Hara, Ted Berrigan, James Schuyler, John Wieners, Anne Waldman, and Alice Notley.

To look back over Riley's poetic career is to trace a history of questioning, of disruption and challenge. The 1985 collection *Dry Air* gathers poems from earlier books, including *Marxism for Infants* (1977), *No Fee* (1978), and *Some Poems* (1982), the latter two representing collaborations with Mulford. The collaborative project is inherently feminist here, seeking to challenge the notion of individual authorship as masculine in its claim to an autonomous imagination. Instead, collaboration is explored as a method of encountering the self in relation to other selves. In general, the poems of *Dry Air* take on the social and cultural forces that shape the gendered self, and they ask how language can affect these structures. In this sense, these poems overtly engage with Riley's political and philosophical backgrounds, while exploring ways poetry and its languages might enter the texture of the public world without depending solely on polemics. Often Riley (and Mulford/Riley) make use of familiar narratives, layering them in unexpected ways to expose damaging ideas kept in place by language. For example, in a poem like "Affections Must Not", economic ideas, rather than seen as existing only in some separate world of markets and public exchange, are explored in relation to romantic notions of love. The poem's title signals its negotiation with the traditional love poem, the poem of "affections." Certainly, both romantic love and conventional praise of feminine beauty and virtue receive a dashing here, as narratives of home and motherhood are shown to issue "straight out of colonial history, master and slave". The poem's speaker, a housewife, imagines an alternative narrative, presented formally in the poem as an alternative grammar: "I. neglect. the. house." The punctuation allows each word to stand separately while on the same line, a grammatical change breaking, as it were, the "wires which run to & fro between love and economics"; breaking the poetic line between "I" and "house," and so gesturing toward a break between love and economics.

This kind of grammatical play, characteristic of many of these poems, is not mere rhetorical trickery but an attempt to explore the power of representation, both to circumscribe us and to liberate us. "A note on sex and 'the reclaiming of language'" presents a female subject facing the difficulty of self-representation in a system of culture and language that has represented women as the "not-you", the Other. Rather than assuming an essentialized "woman", the poem tackles the process by which womanhood is constructed. The opening of the poem claims that the necessary task is "e.g. to write 'she' and for that to be a statement / of fact only and not a strong image / of everything which is not-you, which sees you". As the poem's overlays of narrative suggest, the woman it presents understands herself within the discourses or descriptions that allow others to "see" her. Employing a storyline in which a woman (called "The Savage") returns home from a trip, the poem places this ostensibly ordinary narrative within the context of imperialist conquest and the domination of nature:

> The Savage is flying back home from the New Country
> in native-style dress with a baggage of sensibility
> to gaze on the ancestral plains with the myths thought up
> and dreamed in her kitchens as guides
> > > She will be discovered

Later, we discover that "the new land is colonised, though its prospects are empty" and "The Savage Weeps as landing at the airport / she is asked to buy wood carvings, which represent herself". Just as public myths enter the kitchen "as guides", the private woman is neither separate from nor immune to the demeaning definitions of the "feminine" attributed by private, public, historical, and literary spheres. The language of the poem, in evoking various narratives, seeks an alternative for the "she" to the pejorative representations available to her, and suggests that the meaning "flocking densely around the words seeking a way / any way in between the gaps" occurs not through mimesis but through

those "gaps"; the gaps, that is, made apparent when seemingly disparate narratives (travel, domestic, imperial) are brought together and their interconnections become evident.

Dry Air considers the role of institutions of family, religion, nationalism, and morality in defining gender identity. How does the "I" perceive itself, much less represent itself, in the midst of culture's dominant images of women? And how do structures of language take part in advancing conventions of gender that privilege men? And yet in asking these questions, in seeking out textual alternatives, Riley also explores the question of whether linguistic experimentation can backfire. Self-consciously registering its own artifice, Riley's poetry is invariably alive to the danger that avant-garde experimentation can produce a poetry as precious and as private as the traditional lyric. Following from this, Riley continually registers a need to connect linguistic experimentation with an awareness of history, economics, and social forces. A poem like "Ah So" suggests that the lyric voice speaking to itself cannot be politically effective ("Speaking apart, I hear my voice run on . . . / disturb the text; you don't disturb the world"), while also suggesting that language is not in and of itself oppositional. In a world where men have both money and power, the material subordination of women is not merely a matter of linguistic construction, as we see in the final line of "Ah so": "I found some change in my trouser pocket, like / a man". To be a subject is to be an economic agent is to be a man. How can textual manipulation effectively challenge such a system?

Taking up this question, *Mop Mop Georgette* (1993) moves in more experimental directions. The page itself is theatre for the visual appearance of these poems, often set within large, dense looking blocks of long lines that convey a visceral heaviness interrupted by other poems appearing as scant vertical spears on the whiteness of the page. The sense of the visual page as a white field marked by language is enhanced by the book's physical shape, a six-inch by six-inch square. The shape of the page encourages a visual rhythm from poem to poem, or among a single poem's sections. Riley fills some pages almost to the brim in every direction, stretching lines to fill the space squarely, while other poems rest like slender ladders raised along the left margin of the page to invite the release – or pressure – of whiteness. There is an intimacy and an invitation to the handheld size of the book, although once we enter its visual and verbal rhythms, the way through is anything but small.

Indeed, the poems in this volume ride on enormous energies, accrued through shifting and unsettling movements of language and tone, through collisions between poetic convention and popular culture, cacophonies woven by the myriad voices of a speaking "I". Take a poem like "Lure, 1963". There, Riley splices popular song lyrics into lines dripping with sensually charged colours, developing a somewhat hallucinatory wordscape through which the "I" wanders, bumping up against fragmented love lyrics:

> Navy near-black cut in with lemon, fruity bright lime green.
> I roam around around around around acidic yellows, globe
> oranges burning, slashed cream, huge scarlet flowing
> anemones, barbaric pink singing, radiant weeping When
> will I be loved?   Flood, drag to papery long brushes
> of deep violet, that's where it is, indigo, oh no, it's in
> his kiss. Lime brilliance. Obsessive song. Ink tongues.

Threading the disjunctive syntax with linking echoes and patterns of sound, Riley inserts popular song refrains that act as road markers for the speaker's "lure" into the erotically evocative "floating space" of "welling rose and milk", a "burning place of / whitest shores, a wave out on the ocean [that] could never / move that way, flower, swell, don't ever make her blue." The song lyrics hang like anchors in this almost incoherent but appealing "swell"; yet, by the poem's end, their stability reads as an obstacle, or at the least, a distraction into habitual expression. The last three lines suggest abrupt shifts between multiple voices within the "I," voices inflected not only by different languages of "love" but attentive to the force of formulaic expression (the song fragments) to make unintelligible – unhearable – other languages of sensual desire: "Oh yes I'm the great pretender. Red lays a stripe of darkest / green on dark. My need is such I pretend too much, I'm / wearing. And you're not listening to a word I say." How do we hear one another, the poem seems to ask, outside the habits of language that order and familiarize experience but reduce complexity to formulae. The question of how or whether we can recognize and negotiate these formulae or scripts – rather than erroneously think we can ever escape them – runs through this volume, as in "Misremembered Lyric," which begins by musing, "A misremembered lyric: a soft catch of its song / whirrs in my throat".

Typically, then, Riley's poetry seeks to break through habits of language use that enclose meaning in stale forms; moreover, her poetry asks us to engage in reading practices alternative to the linear forms of logic that seem almost natural to us but that are themselves as artificial as any construction of language. When we read the newspaper to get information, we tend to disregard the role of its language in shaping our understanding of that information; in such a context, language seems transparent, a natural conduit for content. Riley's poetry clouds that transparency and forces us to confront language as a material medium that shapes us as much as we shape it. Riley's work concurrently thrills and struggles with the notion that we can never purely access either a "self" or "experience" prior to or outside of language.

So, we are plunged headlong into language in work that is often about language itself and its forms, particularly its poetic forms. A density and accumulation of detail drives these poems through alternately heady and disorienting and stunning swathes of expression, where as readers, we are caught in the energy of words brought forth with evocative precision and generous fullness. These poems invite rereading – once we catch our breath – as a total immersion into the palpable, visceral, material medium of words. Poetic conventions and genres yield to the pressure of such immersion. The lyric as a place of private utterance, an expression and revelation of a true self, gives way to a reconsideration of the relation of the lyric to the voice speaking it, reversing the notion of a self in control of expression. "A Shortened Set" unfurls as a long poem tense with tracing the writer's anxious confrontation with the viability of a "unique" voice. In movements typical of Riley's poetry, the poem constructs itself through familiar devices – poetic language, imagery, metaphor, etc. – only then to pull the rug out from under itself.

The refusal to separate linguistic constructs from material contexts underlies Riley's more vexed contemplations of the lyric, as in "Disintegrate Me", which experiments with a dispersal of self in language and then reflects back upon that experiment. After a dazzling succession of shifts between subjectivity, romantic idiom, and metacommentary on these very shifts, the poem ends by wondering whether this denial of self, posed as an avoidance of responsibility, is also a denial of necessary agency: "if I understood / my own extent of blame then that would prove me agent".

In its investigation of the lyric and the lyric speaker, Riley's poetry continually questions the relationship of the self to the social and political world. "Laibach Lyrik: Slovenia, 1991", the opening poem of *Mop Mop Georgette*, places lyric utterance squarely within political reality. Here Riley draws upon, while also wrenching out of shape, the transcendent urge of conventional lyricism. Opening with a pastoral evocation of a "[b]reathless" vision of the "milky sheen of birch trees / stepping forward", "cream fields", and "wreaths of raspberry smoke / [that] pat the steady sky", the poem violently halts itself with the command to "cut the slavonics now". We come to realize that we are in a land once labeled as Yugoslavia, and that the pastoral, romanticized imagery of "herdsmen, clattering", who "wheel about / the plains in scarlet" covers over the ideology of nationalism and civil war. The pretty poem is not enough here. The problem of representation comes immediately to the fore in this second section, and the question of how to position and represent one's self intensifies with the pressure of national identity, and with the realization that the category of nationality is shifting:

> Entering Yugoslavia we aren't there, we are straight into Slovenia instead
> late at night, frozen, instantly crazy with obsessive and terrible tenderness
> again, unable to find my passport. Napoléon, sauveur of Illyria! Whose
> monument in Ljubljana spells out in gleams of gold calligraphy, Our Liberty.
> Here videos of the summer bombings, entitled the Triumph of Slovenia, or
> How a Nation Awoke, are wrapped in paper jackets showing fighter planes
> with yellow extension-lead cables, mortar smoke, on stalls with t-shirts,
> logos of the state. The country restaurant pipes a first-time go
> at national music to its dining rooms, unclear what that should sound like;
> oompah Bavarian results, mortifying to the city friends, who disconnect
> its speakers, drawing down a ruddy glare of sausages, peasant style.

The general need to represent a national history as well as the ideological bias underlying any version of a history – communicated here by the videos of summer bombings that are renamed in jingoistic rhetoric – is telling on individuals also. Thus, "In London / temporary exiles meet, some in despair about their forced new names /others worn down with dislocation, with explaining histories". These "explaining histories" question the rhetoric of nationalism. One voice asks, "Who says I must be 'Bosnian' now. / I grew up Yugoslavian". Another voice ambivalently asserts the political necessity of a language of nationalism arising out of material circumstances: "the deaths of twenty thousand make me this / that I don't want to be. But that blood lost means I must take that name – / though not that politics – must be, no not a nationalist, yet ambiguously Croatian". The poem's splicing of various voices, including the poet's, that claim or assert an "I" at the individual level or a "we" on the national level, creates a tension between unre-flective ideals of identity and discursive systems that "shape us".

Throughout *Mop Mop Georgette*, the questions and problems of agency posed by "Laibach Lyrik" or "Disintegrate Me" reoccur, overtly and subtly drawing from and forcing issues of gender. The poem "Dark Looks" opens with a fashionable dismissal of the author – "Who anyone is or I is nothing to the work" – to evoke a gender-coded dilemma: "The writer / properly should be the last person that the reader or the listener need think about / yet the poet with her signature stands up trembling, grateful, mortally embarassed / and especially embarassing to herself, patting her hair and twittering If, if only / I need not have a physical appearance! To be sheer air, and mousseline!" This poem rides on shifts in tone and voice that mimic ways of speaking and writing that define author and woman as mutually exclusive categories: "then pat me more, Conventry / to fall from anglocatholic clouds of drifting we's high tones of feeling / down to microscopic horror scans of tiny shiny surfaces rammed up against the nose . . .". As "high tones" fall to more earthly perspectives, the speaker wonders what the "lyric person" can be, and what her relation to readers might be:

> . . . The only point of holding up my blood is if you'd think So what?
> We've all got some of that: since then you'd each feel better; less apart. – Hardly:
> it's more for me to know that I have got some, like a textbook sexual anxiety
> while the social-worker poet in me would like her revenge for having been born and left.
> What forces the lyric person to put itself on trial though it must stay rigorously uninteresting?
> does it count on its dullness to seem human and strongly lovable; a veil for the monomania
> which likes to feel itself helpless and touching at times? Or else it backs off to get sassy
> since arch isn't far from desperate: So take me or leave me. No, wait, I didn't mean leave
> me, wait, just don't – or don't flick and skim to the foot of a page and then get up to go –

Ending the poem with a dash, Riley accentuates the ongoing relation between the page, the poem, the poet, and the reader that her work seeks to explore.

Riley's work encourages an incessant confrontation with language. Her interplay of connective impulses creates not an intellectually solipsistic poetry, but an engaged, inviting and weblike texture of language that catches and contains us all.

Like a Lily Daché Hat

MARK FORD

"WIGGING IN, WIGGING OUT", begins "Trip", the first of a series of poems James Schuyler composed in 1975 during a two-month hospitalisation in Payne Whitney, the psychiatric unit of New York Hospital; "when I stop to think / the wires in my head / cross: kaboom". The poem's twenty-one short lines summarise Schuyler's troubled psychiatric history with unusual directness:

> How
> many trips
> by ambulance (five,
> count them five),
> claustrated, pill addiction,
> in and out of mental
> hospitals,
> the suicidalness (once
> I almost made it)
> but – I go on?
> Tell you all of it?
> I can't. When I think
> of that, that at

only fifty-one, I
Jim the Jerk, am
still alive and breathing
deeply, that I think
is a miracle.

Schuyler in fact stayed "alive and breathing" a further sixteen years, during which he wrote much of his best poetry, an enchanting, hilarious novel called *What's For Dinner?* (1978), and achieved something like cult status among America's poetic cognoscenti. "I like his poetry so much", wrote Elizabeth Bishop in a late letter, "& I have never told him so, nor seen him, & know next to nothing about him". "Your work makes up an 'underground movement' all by itself!" declared Ted Berrigan. When Schuyler finally gave a poetry reading in 1988, having always refused before on account of his extreme shyness, the queue for tickets stretched several deep around the block.

Schuyler was born in Chicago in 1923, but grew up mainly in Washington D.C. and East Aurora, a small town near Buffalo in upstate New York. He later compared his home-life with his mother and stepfather to "a novel by Dostoyevsky". He attended a small college in West Virginia called Bethany, where he fared dismally and left without a degree, mainly because he spent nearly all his time playing bridge. In 1943 he joined the Navy, and saw action while on convoy duty in the North Atlantic; the following year, however, he went AWOL in New York for several weeks, and at the hearing that followed his arrest his homosexuality was revealed. He was branded "undesirable", and discharged from further naval duties.

Schuyler didn't begin writing poetry until the early 1950s. He travelled to Europe in 1947 with the vague idea of developing into a *New Yorker*-style short story writer. He spent two years there, mainly in Italy, with his partner of the time, Bill Aalto, a specialist in guerrilla warfare who had fought on the side of the Republic in the Spanish Civil War. Schuyler and Aalto visited Auden and Chester Kallman on Ischia, and for a while Schuyler worked as Auden's secretary, typing up the manuscript of *Nones*: "Well, if this is poetry", he later recalled thinking as he pecked away, "I'm certainly never going to write any myself". Their Ischian idyll ended when the volatile Aalto – whose right hand had been blown off by a hand-grenade during a training session for recruits – attempted to kill Schuyler with a carving knife.

He returned to New York in August of 1949. In the course of the next few years he met Frank O'Hara, John Ashbery, Barbara Guest, and Kenneth Koch. He also suffered his first major manic attack, which took the form of a religious ecstasy: he was convinced he'd had a long conversation with the Virgin Mary, who informed him that Judgement Day was nigh. He was sent to Bloomingdale mental hospital in White Plains, and it was during his three-month stay there that his earliest poems were written. Further breakdowns and hospitalisations followed in 1956, in 1961, in 1971 (on this occasion he believed he was Jesus Christ and spent hours carefully washing dollar bills in the bathtub, then pegging them on a clothes line to dry), in 1973, 1975, 1976, 1977, 1978, 1979, and finally 1985. He rarely had any money, and lived mainly with friends such as Fairfield Porter – whose wife Anne once joked that Schuyler came for a visit and ended up staying eleven years – Kenward Elmslie and Darragh Park. In the late seventies he shuttled between psychiatric units, nursing homes, flea-pit hotels and rooming-houses – in one of which he nearly died in a fire he caused himself by falling asleep holding a lit cigarette. Finally, in 1979, a grant from the

Frank O'Hara Foundation enabled him to settle in the Chelsea Hotel on West 23rd Street, and be looked after by a series of paid assistants.

Schuyler's work is nearly always considered in the context of "The New York School", the label dreamed up by John Bernard Myers, who was the director of the Tibor de Nagy Gallery and published the early work of Ashbery, Koch, and O'Hara in a series of Tibor de Nagy poetry pamphlets in the '50s. Schuyler's early poems would have appeared in this series too, but it seems he suddenly lost faith in his poethood, and then – this was in the run-up to his breakdown of 1961 – took to blaming Frank O'Hara for undermining his self-esteem. O'Hara was, in many ways, everything Schuyler wasn't: brash, prolific, confident, talkative, robust, always the centre of attention, and any number of people's best friend: "and it was given to me", O'Hara writes in a 1954 poem dedicated to Schuyler, "as the soul is given the hands / to hold the ribbons of life!" The more passive Schuyler rarely gives the impression of having a firm grip on the ribbons, let alone the reins, of life, and the dilemmas his poetry ponders tend to be quotidian and specific: "There is a hornet in the room", begins his superb elegy for O'Hara, "Buried at Springs",

> and one of us will have to go
> out the window into the late
> August midafternoon sun. I
> won. There is a certain challenge
> in being humane to hornets
> but not much.

Characteristically the poem alludes only obliquely to his friend's violent death in a gruesome accident on Fire Island in 1966: "a faintly clammy day", it concludes,

> like wet silk
> stained by one dead branch
> the harsh russet of dried blood.

While O'Hara loved singing the praises of "life-giving vulgarity", Schuyler was all reticence and tact. It has even been suggested by David Lehman in his study of the group, *The Last Avant-Garde: The Making of the New York School of Poets* (1998), that O'Hara's death "acted as a sort of imaginative liberation for Schuyler"; it allowed him, Lehman argues, to assume "O'Hara's project and adapt it to his own sensibility". His first collection, *Freely Espousing*, was published in 1969, long after Koch, Ashbery, and O'Hara had become, if not household names, reasonably well-known in American poetry circles.

Certainly O'Hara and Schuyler's representations of the urban could hardly be more different. In poem after poem O'Hara charts his love of Manhattan, and his fractured, pulsing, open forms seem ways of miming the city's random juxtapositions and erotic and aesthetic energies, its plenitude of choice and almost overwhelming sense of possibility. Even nature is better in the city – "One need never leave the confines of New York to get all the greenery one wishes", he informs us in the prose poem "Meditations in an Emergency", "I can't even enjoy a blade of grass unless I know there's a subway handy, or a record store or some other sign that people do not totally *regret* life". Schuyler, on the other hand, often figures himself yearning for the joys of rural calm, as in the short diary poem, "The Morning", written soon after he moved into the Chelsea Hotel:

                I
almost accept the fact
that I am not in
the country, where I
long to be, but in
this place of glass
and stone – and metal,
let's not forget
metal – where traffic sounds and the day
is well begun. So
be it, morning.

Both O'Hara and Schuyler – much more than Koch, Ashbery, or Guest – liked to fill their poems with references; to friends, to social events, to everyday activities such as making toast or shopping or eating lunch, and to their favourite painters, musicians, and writers. O'Hara's literary allusions tend to be to avant-garde French and Russian poets, such as René Char, Pierre Reverdy ("My heart is in my / pocket, it is Poems by Pierre Reverdy"), Paul Éluard, Mayakovsky, Marcelin Pleynet, Apollinaire, and so on; Schuyler, meanwhile, always seems to be immersed in Trollope ("we settle down / to read; he, a Ross / MacDonald, me *Phineas / Redux*") or Virginia Woolf, or in Herrick or Traherne or Vaughan or Tennyson or Lady Mary Wortley Montague or Gilbert White or Vita Sackville-West or the Sitwells. "I'm reading", he writes in "A Few Days" (1985),

                    Osbert Sitwell's autobiography
            stitched in brocade. I
    read a page, then rush back to my poem. I would once have
            thought that Sitwell
    was "influencing" me. I'm too me for that. Poor trembling
            Osbert, suffering from
    Parkinson's disease. I met him at a party Wystan gave for
            them. John was
    dashing tears from his eyes: "What's wrong?" "I just met
            Edith Sitwell". Tender
    heart. Edith looked less like her photograph. She was
            creased and had that
    famous nose.

These references testify to a deep and intriguing Anglophilia. Schuyler never in fact visited England, but in the '50s he worked for several years at an English specialist bookstore, the Periscope-Holliday on East 54th street, and in later life grew into a devotee of magazines such as *The Countryman, The Tatler, The Field,* and *Private Eye,* which he used to buy from an import magazine shop on Broadway. One poem of his, "The Fireproof Floors of Witley Court (English Songs and Dances)" is based on extracts from back issues of *Country Life* ("Fry's Cocoa! The word / means food of the gods . . . Swan and Edgar / Good linen / Swan and Edgar / Good linen") while "Under the Hanger", which is three pages long, consists entirely of phrases lifted from the journals of Gilbert White:

Wood lark whistles. Hogs carry straw.
Sky lark sings.
Young cucumber swells.
Frogs croak: spawn abounds.
Cold & black. Harsh, hazy day.
Backward apples begin to blow.
Frost, sun, fog, rain, snow. Bunting twitters.
No dew, rain, rain, rain.
Swans flounce & dive.
Chilly & dark.
Dark & spitting. Indian flowers in Dec'r!
Ground very wet. The nightingale sings . . .

Although he never owned a garden, in the late '60s Schuyler opened an account with Landsman's in Herefordshire, a "Specialist Postal Bookshop for Farmers and Gardeners", from whom he used to acquire manuals that enabled him to keep up with the latest in English horticultural fashions. One of his most delicate late poems describes an English rose called "Princess Di"; this poem, although composed over a decade before the fatal crash in the Parisian underpass, with hindsight seems eerily prophetic. The rose, given him by his secretary while he convalesces in hospital, resembles a Georg Arends hybrid:

silvery, pink
larger, with sharply
pointed petals, the only
rose to do so (I thought,
I imagined) what joy
to see it recur in Princess
Di named for we all know
who and the Chinese lady
heard what I said when
she asked and she said,
"Princess Diana the Princess
Diana" and as the days
passed and you came
to escort me home and
the rose I had watched
grown fat and soft
expired as I left
and I thought, "Beautiful
Princess, farewell!"

Schuyler was particularly fond of English diarists, and his own Diary, which was published by Black Sparrow in 1997, is full of references to such as Kilvert (whose *magnum opus* Schuyler read "many many times"), Dorothy Wordsworth, the Bloomsbury diarist Frances Partridge, and the eighteenth-century parson James Woodeforde, whose five-volume journal records the minutiae of daily life in Western Longeville, Norfolk. Schuyler also loved the work of memoirists such as Constance Spry, the pre-eminent London society florist of her day and author of botanical tomes such as *Come into the Garden, Cook* (1942) and *Favourite Flowers* (1959), Harry Daley, a policeman from Lowestoft who had an affair with E. M. Forster and published his reminiscences in *This Small Cloud* (1986), and Arthur Randell, author of *Fenway Railwaymen* (1968), of which, Schuyler observes, "it might be possible to say it contains not one memorable word, and therefore has a pleasant clarity, like a clear glass of water". Other favourite writers mentioned include Malcolm Elwin (author of *Victorian Wallflowers*, 1934), Iris Origo, Sydney Smith, Andrew Young, William Cobbett, William Robinson, Patrick Leigh-Fermor, Richard Jeffries, and the nineteenth-century English historian of the law, F.W. Maitland, from whose "Leet and Tourn" (1888), Schuyler quotes a sentence which struck him as particularly "beautiful":

> To the student of manorial rolls by far the most interesting franchise is the "court leet or view of frank-pledge", because it is very common, because it has great importance in the history of society, because its origin is extremely obscure; so obscure that we may be rash in speaking about it; still a little may be ventured.

A little may be ventured on the subject of Schuyler's delightfully camp enjoyment of a certain kind of Englishness, and its importance to his development as a writer. He was not, it must be said, much interested in twentieth-century English poetry, and shared with the Beats and the Objectivists and the Black Mountaineers as well as with his fellow New York School poets an energizing contempt for the conservative East Coast poetic establishment, "the campus dry-heads", as he once characterised them, "who wishfully descend tum-ti-tumming from Yeats out of Graves with a big kiss for Mother England". His earliest writings, collected in *The Home Book 1951–1970* (1977), reveal a slightly uneasy determi-nation to experiment with the kind of goofy Surrealist-inspired disjunctions characteristic of the early work of Koch, O'Hara, and Ashbery. Schuyler's first publication, however, was the short fiction *Alfred and Guinevere* (1958, reissued 2001), an elusive, haunting fusion of the clichés of small-town American novels, movies, and children's stories with the English comedy of manners as written by such as E. F. Benson, Henry Green, Ronald Firbank, Ivy Compton-Burnett, and George and Weedon Grossmith. *Alfred and Guinevere* is almost entirely in dialogue, and mainly very simple dialogue, since its principal characters, the siblings Alfred and Guinevere, are around eight and ten years old respectively. But beneath the whimsical repartee and kiddie joshing and one-upmanship circulate complex emotional currents the novel refuses ever to define or drag to the surface. In this, it greatly resembles Jane Bowles's *Two Serious Ladies*, published fifteen years earlier, which also uses manners and dialogue to develop an elliptical narrative that continually undermines our expectations and unsettles our perspective on events and characters. Bowles and Schuyler both, I think, found in the English society novel a means of side-stepping what might be called its antithesis, the Great American Novel, which must somehow include and interpret as much of the American past, present, and future as possible, and ideally should create a new fictional form for itself to boot. Schuyler, who worshipped Bowles, recorded with delight in his diary her Firbankian response to a publisher explaining why she didn't want her novel reissued: "it has its own little following, like a Lily Daché hat". Manners and fashion here serve to mock the very idea the book could be anything superior to a minor or cult classic.

"So modest", Schuyler writes of Darwin, whose autobiography he has just started, in "Empathy and New Year" (the New Year in question was 1968), "so innocent, so pleased at

/ the surprise that *he* / should turn out to be *him*". Modesty is a crucial aspect of Schuyler's poetics, and so is the pleased and surprised discovery of one's individuality – the sense one can be too "me" to be influenced by others. This notion of developing into a particular, determined identity runs interestingly – and modestly – against the grain of the standard American ideal of the self as fluid, beyond definition, and somehow infinite. "Encompass worlds but never try to encompass me", admonishes Whitman in "Song of Myself". O'Hara also frequently explores a Whitmanesque vision of the poet instantly metamorphosing into whatever he imagines or identifies with, as in the litany of selves that succeed each other in "In Memory of My Feelings": "I am a Chinaman climbing a mountain / I am a child smelling his father's underwear I am an Indian / sleeping on a scalp . . ." O'Hara is of course on one level mocking the whole nationalist ideology of self-reliance – "What land is this, so free?" he asks caustically a few lines later – but the poem's collage of discourses and compendium of images also situate it squarely in the tradition of the American song of one's self. Schuyler clearly needed to evade the implications of the carpetbag form of the American long poem as it developed from Whitman to Pound to Williams to O'Hara. What he found in the journals of such as Kilvert and Woodforde and Gilbert White was not only a form of pastoral, but a way of writing that concentrated on the everyday, and in which things were described for their own sakes. They in turn suggested how his own poetry might avoid dealing with what John Ashbery calls, in "Daffy Duck in Hollywood", "the big / Vaguer stuff" – metaphysics and symbolism and issues of self-figuration – and instead accommodate the random trivialities of experience without either loading them with significance, or making them seem mere illustrations of chaos and contingency. Indeed the English diarists offered a template both for long poems such as "Hymn to Life", "The Morning of the Poem", and "A Few Days", and for the seemingly artless day to day bulletins offered by short poems such as "The Morning".

A number of these short pieces are simply titled by their dates: "8 / 12 / 70", "June 30, 1974", "Dec. 28, 1974", "October 5, 1981", and many start out, like diary entries, recording a change in the weather:

> After two rainy days, a sunny one
> of cloud curds breaking up in blue . . .
>
> ("Evenings in Vermont")

> Awoke to rain
> and mist, down
> there in Gospel
> Hollow: a cloud
> that frayed and
> flowed uphill
> as the drizzling day
> wore on . . .
>
> ("Awoke")

> Then it snowed. I
> saw it when I let
> the dog out into
> the dark yard, fat
> damp flakes, ag-
> glomerations of
> many flakes . . .
>
> ("Afterward")

Schuyler's observations, like those lifted from Gilbert White's journals in "Under the Hanger", tend to be low-key, accurate, and mundane, "threaded", as he puts it in "Hymn to Life", "with dailiness":

> Another day, the sun
> Comes out from behind unbuttoned cloud underclothes – gray with use –
> And bud scales litter the sidewalks. A new shop is being built,
> An old one refurbished.

Much of his poetry is written in either very short or very long lines: either extreme functions somewhat as the continuous use of dialogue in *Alfred and Guinevere* – one feels afloat in a medium wholly absorbed in the specifics of what it's presenting but which refuses to offer a "tum-ti-tumming" framework which make explicit why either he or we should be interested in the opening of a new shop or a change in the weather. The effect is very different from that of the *culte de moi* enacted in O'Hara's "I do this, I do that" poems, which radiate both an insouciant coterie glamour, and an urgent, thrilling excitement at being in the thick of the action:

> It is 12.20 in New York and I am wondering
> if I will finish this in time to meet Norman for lunch
> ah lunch! I think I am going crazy
> what with my terrible hangover and the weekend coming up
> at excitement-prone Kenneth Koch's . . .

Schuyler's descriptions of life in the city never make us feel his friends are more gifted than anyone else's or that Manhattan is the centre of the universe – indeed he often seems to wish he were somewhere else: "Lincoln, the Lincolnshire wolds, the Peak District, Ely, the gardens at Chatsworth", he ruminates in "The Morning of the Poem" on receiving a letter from friends holidaying in England, "I wish I had been with you". More fervently still he wishes he'd been at Rodmell in March of 1941

> to parlay with Virginia Woolf
> when she was about to take
> that fatal walk: "I know you're
> sick, but you'll be well
> again: trust me: I've been there."

Neither Woolf nor Schuyler fashioned from their "suicidalness" an expressionist drama of anguish, confession, or revenge. Even at his most fragile, in, say, "The Payne Whitney Poems", Schuyler seems as interested in the weather as in his own condition, while his long poems continually reflect upon – and ground themselves in – the cycles of seasonal change. In the best of Schuyler's work the forces of time, language, and nature come to seem as helplessly and inextricably intertwined as in the image with which he concludes his salute to the "poor lovely lady" whose writings – in particular her diaries – he adored:

> Angular Virginia Woolf, for whom
> words came streaming
> like clouded yellows over the downs.

Reviews

Misty in Roots –
Chinese Poetry after Mao

JULIA LOVELL

ALTHOUGH A KEEN amateur poet himself, Mao Zedong shared with Plato a deep suspicion of what other poets might get up to in his Republic. In 1942, Mao demanded that "workers in literature and art should . . . be 'oxen' for the proletariat and the masses". "There is", he pronounced, "no such thing as art for art's sake . . . art that is detached from or independent of politics. Proletarian literature, and art . . . are, as Lenin said, cogs and wheels in the whole revolutionary machine." Indeed, after the founding of the People's Republic of China in 1949, Mao attempted to abolish poets altogether, launching mass poetry movements in which the peasants, workers, and soldiers were exhorted to start doing it for themselves. The Westernised style of new poetry introduced during China's modern literary revolution of the 1910s–1920s was shunned in favour of proletarian Folk Song forms. This 1958 specimen showcases the literary fruits of Mao's campaign: "Big character posters / Big character posters / They're like stars / As well as cannon".

Maoist strictures reached their height in the Cultural Revolution (1966–76), during which openly reading or writing almost anything at all was seen as a sign of dangerous ideological subversion. After Mao's death in 1976, however, it was underground poetry that led the rebellion against the Maoist deadlock on literature. In 1968, Mao displaced millions of urban intellectuals, many of them high school students, to the countryside to be "reformed" by labouring with the peasants. The social chaos that resulted provided many of the "sent-down youth" with an unintended degree of intellectual freedom. Translations of forbidden foreign writers – T. S. Eliot, the French Symbolists, Beckett – were secretly passed between young poets who would later spearhead literary innovation in the post-Mao thaw, such as Bei Dao (b. 1949), Mang Ke (b. 1950) and Gu Cheng (1956–93).

If the Cultural Revolution provided the context in which these poets' literary sensibilities were stimulated, the political bankruptcy of Cultural Revolution Maoism triggered a crisis of faith in Communist authority that would deeply colour their poetry. Bei Dao's 1972 poem "The Answer" clearly demonstrates the defiance felt by him and his peers towards the political power of the state:

> Let me tell you world,
> I – do – not – believe!
> If a thousand challengers lie beneath your feet,
> Count me as number one thousand and one.

Already in contact with each other during the Cultural Revolution, Bei Dao and his fellow underground poets gathered into a more formal grouping following their permanent return to Beijing after 1976. Taking advantage of the political relaxation that made possible the Democracy Wall Movement of 1978–79, Bei Dao and Mang Ke set up an unofficial but highly influential magazine for literature and art: *Jintian* (Today). Proclaiming itself to be a non-political, literary publication – a deeply subversive act in 1970s China – *Jintian* carried for the first time works by experimental poets (Bei Dao, Mang Ke and others) that have since been canonised as emblematic works of the post-Mao literary breakthrough.

By late 1979, however, the end of the first post-Mao political thaw terminated the Mainland publishing run of *Jintian*. Closed down in December, the magazine would not be restarted until Bei Dao and many of his original contributors went into Western exile after June 1989. But the underground poetry published in *Jintian* continued to be seen and heard, thanks to its controversial labelling within official literary circles as "Misty" (or obscure) poetry. This new, experimental poetry represented an obvious challenge to the orthodox Communist model, thanks to the poets' open acknowledgement of Western influences, and emphasis on the personal, private, and individual over the political, public, and collective. Theirs was a strongly imagistic poetry, often broken up into short, elliptical stanzas devoid of didactic certainty or kitsch socialist optimism. Take, for example, Gu Cheng's "Feeling":

> The sky is grey
> The road is grey
> The building is grey
> The rain is grey
> In this dead expanse of grey
> Two children walk by
> One bright red
> One pale green

Such poetic intimations that life under socialism was at best monochrome and certainly not glorious technicolour provoked outrage from orthodox critics. Following thirty Maoist years in which absolute clarity of meaning had been essential to political survival, ambiguity was the greatest imaginable heterodoxy. The old guard lambasted the new poetry for being "weird" and "opaque", for its rebellion against the rigid idea of the writer serving the socialist collective of the Chinese people (whoever they might be). "Poetry that cannot be understood, accepted and appreciated by the masses", fumed one orthodox critic, "is either bad poetry or not poetry at all."

Opposition to Misty Poetry climaxed during the 1983 Anti-Spiritual Pollution Campaign, which seemed to spell a chilling return to the mass movements of political persecution characteristic of the Cultural Revolution. But with the abrupt cessation of the campaign in 1984, experimental, non-official poetry, along with its commitment to artistic freedom of expression, gained wider acceptance in official literary circles. Although the Communist literary establishment and the poetic avant-garde would never merge amicably, a greater degree of tolerance between the two now became possible, resulting in increased publishing opportunities for experimental poets.

By 1984, new poetry magazines and collections were burgeoning, heralding the emergence of "New Generation" or "Post-Misty" schools of poetry. While most members of this poetic generation (born principally in the mid-1950s to 1960s) would acknowledge a debt to their Misty predecessors in having forged a creative, intellectual space for experimental poetry, deference to the Misties went little further. Indeed, many of the newer poets placed themselves in conscious opposition to the high-blown, socio-political ideals of the Jintian poets, rallying under the slogan "Down with Bei Dao!"

Although hostile to the politics of Maoist orthodoxy, Misty Poetry itself harboured unmistakably political, even patriotic overtones. Its individualistic voice often expressed a collective sadness at the wounds wrought on China by the Cultural Revolution and a desire for the country to find its way again, as conveyed by Liang Xiaobin's lament to the motherland: "China, my key is lost // Oh my key, / Where are you? // I am determined to search / Hoping to recover you".

Underneath the rebellious nihilism of Bei Dao's "The Answer" lay faith in a heroic, poetic voice capable both of exposing ideological bankruptcy and of forging a powerful aesthetic alternative that was political by implication.

No such faith survived in younger poets, who veered either towards greater opacity and language games that betrayed a deep scepticism in poetry's potential for expressing collective meaning, or towards an anti-heroic, prosaic language aimed at mirroring the imperfections of ordinary life and undermining the lofty ideals of Misty Poetry. Han Dong's (b. 1961) use of a free, colloquial style and dismissal of poetic heroics are well illustrated in "Of Wild Goose Pagoda", a poem ridiculing attempts by modern Chinese poets to emulate their pre-modern predecessors' custom of climbing ivory towers to compose grandiose, elitist poetry:

> What can we now know
> Of Wild Goose Pagoda
> Which many hurry to, from afar
> To climb
> To be heroes
> . . .
> Then they descend
> Enter the street down below
> Are gone in an instant
> . . .
> What can we now know
> Of Wild Goose Pagoda
> Up we climb
> Look all around us
> Then come down again

A more intricate, unconcernedly elitist style was sought by poets such as Xi Chuan (b. 1963) who, in works such as "Darkness", was happy to give free play to his intellectual narrative voice without worrying excessively about its ability to cast light on life's mysteries:

> Distant darkness is a legend, lengthy darkness sleeplessness
> Hold up your torch, what do you see –
> Darkness, infinite darkness
> . . .
> But when you raise the torch there is only infinite darkness
> Only you are left, to listen to the drip of water
> Dew drops are at the window

Since the Tiananmen Uprising of 1989, when many of the *Jintian* grouping of Misty Poets went into Western exile, geographical as much as generational and stylistic factors have divided contemporary Chinese poetry. This fact of exile has led to a sometimes undue politicisation of contemporary Chinese poetry within the West. Despite attempts by Bei Dao, probably the best known exile poet and for years the front-running Chinese candidate for a Nobel Prize, to seek "Forms of Distance" (the title of a 1994 collection) from his political persona, and despite the increasingly inward turn of his poetry by the mid-1990s, he has often been read as a poet of exile, defined by his associations with the 1989 demonstrations. Exile poets have found themselves both helped and constrained by their politicised status in the West, which on the one hand increases their marketability and translation opportunities, but on the other gives them a limited artistic shelf-life, as readers search their writing above all for references to Tiananmen and the Cultural Revolution. The West's tendency to adopt the exile poets as international representatives of China has, moreover, fostered resentment amongst poets remaining in the Mainland, who accuse the exiles of pandering to Western fantasies about a repressive China and of neglecting questions of deeper artistic value.

> Following thirty Maoist years in which absolute clarity of meaning had been essential to political survival, ambiguity was the greatest imaginable heterodoxy. The old guard lambasted the new poetry for being "weird" and "opaque", for its rebellion against the rigid idea of the writer serving the socialist collective of the Chinese people (whoever they might be). "Poetry that cannot be understood, accepted and appreciated by the masses", fumed one orthodox critic, "is either bad poetry or not poetry at all".

Interference from politics, however, was not the only problem faced by Mainland poets in the 1990s. In the 1980s, poetry had played a central role in breaking China and its literature out of the intellectual stranglehold of Maoism. The advance of the Chinese market economy after 1989, however, sidelined all forms of "pure" literature, and no genre suffered more dramatic a demotion than poetry. While the government dismantled the "iron rice-bowl" (the Communist promise of a salary for life to its state-contracted writers), publishing houses looked to their profit margins, away from avant-garde poetry. As novelists and poets alike abandoned "high art" for television writing and business, Zhou Lunyou described in 1993 the demoralising effects of the market economy on creative writing: "The blows of commodities are more gentle, more direct than violence, / More cruel too, pushing the spirit toward total collapse".

This sense of marginality fostered a romantic siege mentality within some poets, provoking a vehement rejection of contemporary Chinese materialism. In certain circles, poetry in the 1990s evolved into a pure, quasi-religious undertaking, loftily detached from the money-grubbing reality of Chinese capitalism. Poets such as Chen Dongdong (b. 1961) expressed this sense of sacred mission in the language of martyrdom: "In order to light the fire of the soul in the realm of the divine, the poet has no choice but to set himself on fire." The image of the poet as a tragic romantic genius doomed to self-sacrifice at the altar of art has been reinforced by the actual suicide of several poets in the past thirteen years, such as the promising young poet Haizi (b. 1964) in 1989 and the exile poet Gu Cheng in 1993.

In many of the survivors of the cult of poetry, however, aversion to these two post-1989 constraints – the Western enthusiasm for political exotica, on the one hand, and the pressures of a commodity economy, on the other – has given rise to a poetry of increased obscurity and opaqueness. Whether written in the Mainland or in exile, Chinese poetry became generally "harder" during the 1990s, glorifying the autonomous, independent voice of the poet. The work of the exile poet Yang Lian (b. 1955) typifies this tendency, flinging together objects and images, and confronting the reader with an abstruse authorial perspective that leaps non-sequentially between disjointed images and mutating forms.

> open mouths   poking from chests to eat meat
> winds blow huge ear-rings of straw
> sharks with sinister intent climb trees behind your back
> climb on the bench of the ocean

A similar indeterminacy and surreal juxtaposition of images feature in the 1992 prose-poem, "Salute", by the Mainland-based poet Xi Chuan:

> The spider intercepts an imperial edict, thus going against the wish of the road.

> In hemp fields, lamps have no rights of residence.

> Someone is about to arrive and knock on the door, sheep are about to appear and roam
> in the meadow . . .

Given this widespread shift towards opacity, it is perhaps unsurprising that by the start of the new millennium, writers of Chinese poetry were thought to outnumber readers. In the two decades since 1979, the aims of the Misty Poets have been largely achieved: to create a space for poetic experimentation within a political culture of literary utilitarianism. In this process, however, poetry has been transformed from the popular frontline of thought liberation, into an isolated, self-enclosed vanguard. In 1979, the inflammatory intellectual impact of an underground poetry magazine such as *Jintian* provoked an official ban. By 2002, although China remains very much a one-party dictatorship, the decline in the public profile of poetry led one avant-garde poet to comment: "Underground poetry barely exists in China any more. Poets can mostly find a way to publish what they want, as long as they pay for the print run themselves". While the government focuses its censorial energies on the Internet and mass media, it remains to be seen what use Chinese poets will come to make of the relative freedom that their efforts have won.

Suggested further reading:
Criticism Bonnie S. McDougall and Kam Louie, *The Literature of China in the Twentieth Century*, Hurst and Company, 1997. Maghiel van Crevel, *Language Shattered: Contemporary Chinese poetry and Duoduo*, Leiden: Research School CNWS, 1996. Michelle Yeh, *Modern Chinese Poetry: Theory and practice since 1917*, Yale University Press, 1991.
Poetry Collections Bei Dao: several collections available in translation, for example *The August Sleepwalker* tr. Bonnie S. McDougall, Anvil Press, 1988. Gu Cheng, *Selected Poems* ed. and tr. by Sean Golden and Chu Chiyu et al., Hong Kong, Chinese University of Hong Kong, 1990. Yang Lian: several collections available in translation, for example *Where the Sea Stands Still* tr. Brian Holton, Bloodaxe, 1999. See also *Renditions* (a Chinese-English translation magazine) no. 37 Spring 1992 for selected "New Generation" poets.

Frankly Espousing

STEPHEN BURT

John James, *Collected Poems*
Salt Publishing, £15.95, ISBN 1876857404

AMONG THE CHALLENGING, sometimes recondite poets long associated with small presses in Cambridge (and widely available only in anthologies like *A Various Art*), the Welsh-born, Bristol-educated John James has long seemed the most personable, the most transparent, and the most fun: he's also the most obviously indebted to a single, durable model – many of his poems, and most of the best, flaunt debts to the verve, flanerie, and diaristic flair of Frank O'Hara, the American poet whose *Lunch Poems* and *Love Poems* made standing still and walking in New York both a method and an ecstatically casual way of life. O'Hara's most recent UK fans (John Stammers comes to mind) have sanded and planed the style he created until the results fit older measures of closure; James presents instead the gregarious, sometimes frustrating style in all its rough charm and sprawl. This big first *Collected* gathers small-press books and chapbooks from *Mmm . . . Ah Yes* (1967) to *Schlegel Eats a Bagel* (1996). It shows not so much a development as a series of phases, which together offer a handful of very good poems, a much larger group of enjoyably quirky lines, and a look at one clever writer's reactions to several locales and changing times.

In its descriptive, short-lined minimalism, *Mmm . . .* owes much not to O'Hara but to William Carlos Williams; "To a Young Art Student in London" explains, in deliberate echoes of Williams' late style,

> Great effort is needed
> to walk across the vast grass
> yet people move
> & we cannot hear them

By the end of the '60s – with the help of some free translations from the Welsh – James had acquired the feel and tone of all his most substantial verse. The poems are diaries, travel journals, descriptions of parts of the world (Cambridge, London, Berlin, Wicklow, rural Wales) as James and his friends have happened to pass through them. They are, also, poems about kinds of attachments to people – erotic attraction, romantic companionship, friendship and loyalty, and the states in between. In a holiday cottage,

> The stars make the room seem cold.
> Faint slumbery breath is picked up from the tumbled bed & the brittle light dwindles to opaque air, to seething particles of dark above the bed.
>
> I unbuckle my belt & lie down gently next my sleeping wife.
>
> ("Blues & Reverie")

Devoted to journeys, excurses, expostulations and improvisations, James has a wonderful flair with the very long sentence, his own way (in Klee's phrase) of "taking a line for a walk":

What most fits us,
like a headscarf say, can be left
behind the arc of a wrist in air & be
retrieved from that current again as if
never let slip.

("With Regard the Matter of Falling")

In "Inventory", a relatively early poem, James makes a declaration: "I desire a tongue /
not distanced from its proper closeness to the feeling brain, / no experimental snail's heart
/ pumping on a weighted string." This establishes the distance between James and his drier,
more consciously experimental Cantabridgian peers; his poems are not scientific
experiments conducted on an unwilling dictionary, but records, for good or ill, of his own
experience, making its traces available to anyone who pays enough attention. The self-
mockingly titled "Poem of Inevitable September, or, I'm a City Boy at Heart" lets all the
resulting (O'Hara-esque) virtues show: these include speedy long lines, longer sentences,
intentional tonal misfires, and comic incongruities which (all together) sustain the illusion
that James is actually talking, right now, to you:

Maybe we have just realised
it's all more difficult than we'd allowed for,
basking in each other's vigour and the sun's, a
couple of repleted cats, but we aren't
cats & I refuse to eat all that badly cooked rice:
what I make of the situation is what I make of the situation.

Though he can spare more time for the mountains than O'Hara ever did, James is indeed
a city boy, given to quick-change moods and urbane evasions, regularly "in need of /
some elegant vulgarity". O'Hara's play of campy or loose-fitting adjectives – set delightedly, and
sometimes delightfully, in between praise and mock-praise – also finds a good home in
James' lines: "How can the nobly tall / look fragile as an ice-skater?" ("Coda to the
Immediately Preceding Poems"). Such whimsically misplaced similes became, during the
1970s, one of James' specialities:

this morning
has all the insistence
of reiterated financial
difficulties
& is hence
PRIVATE & CONFIDENTIAL…

("Striking the Pavilion of Zero")

I must have fallen into a thornbush
or the typical anonymity of Lowestoft
which we like
falls around your shoulders
like a cold shower of eels

("War")

James shares both O'Hara's sense that poems should be real speech-acts directed at real people, and his consequent belief that poetry *qua* poetry must not be all that important: "I must urinate, cut my nails – / Will the real work of poetry ever have such refining effects?" This sense of unimportance prevents the poet from taking his work too seriously, and, sometimes, from taking it seriously enough – some poems read like incomplete first drafts, or like fragments James prefers not to assemble. "Sometimes I think I'm just another little bit / of River Avon driftwood well who isn't?" James asks with surprising gravity: he aims for flux rather than fixity, immediacy rather than aesthetic distance, so insistently that his casual manner can become unnerving in its persistence.

James' work darkened, and grew more political, around 1978: not coincidentally, those years also saw his most overt and extensive use of music, from Satie to Bob Dylan and beyond. *Toasting* (1979) tries to approximate Anglo-Jamaican musicians' "continuous dub / echo & dub", approximating, too, their protest and their Utopian politics: "working away in a miniature Babylon in the muddy lowlands / north of the city can be hard you know?" *A Former Boiling* (1978) goes even further in its contemporaneity: its first few pages comprise rhythmic echoes, interpretations, and verbal sequelae to the Human League's creepy, confrontational first single, "Being Boiled". In making his poetry so clearly unfinished (both in the sense "not polished" and in the sense "without a firm conclusion") the James of the late 1970s ploughed the same ground as some of that era's post-punks: Mark Perry's Alternative TV, for example, incorporated extended dub, atonal wind instruments, and near-silence into what began as self-mocking rock, and tried hard to erase the boundary between the makers of art and their imagined audience.

James' work of the past ten years has grown less ambitious and perhaps less consequential. Some of its strongest passages are spare translations or adaptations of pre-modern lyric from other languages, especially Welsh. Much of the rest amounts to briefest-possible daily notations and mock-concrete in-jokes. Occasionally these minimal poems achieve a kind of perfection – consider "From the Welsh": "a crispy leaf / torn away in air / old already / born this year".

Other short work depends entirely on its references. The one-line poem "Gender" reads "Denise is a very secretive people & so am I". If I read the poem correctly, James wants to praise the subtle Cambridge poet and feminist thinker Denise Riley, while mocking generalizations about "peoples" (the Irish, the Nigerians, women, men). "Skip," on the other hand – "o Jocasta keep my arm in plaster" – I don't get at all: it's not the only place in this large *oeuvre* where I feel as if I'd opened someone else's mail. (Certain poems literally include someone else's mail: one offers the entire postal address for the poet Barry MacSweeney.) Such poems both record and produce what James calls "that / they're-in-there & you're-out-here feeling"; O'Hara's lesser work, as James must know, can produce the same quandary.

James often writes poems, parts of poems, or whole books in discrete page-sized sections, some titled or numbered, many not. More than in most poets, the sections that make up one book, or one poem, seem truly separable; some would be just as good as independent poems, and some seem connected only by chance or temporal proximity – James happened to have both these feelings on the same day, or in sight of the same mountain or railway. The book-length series thus represents, for James, a sort of temptation, since in it he need not think of any unit (lyric, argumentative or otherwise) as an actual or potential whole – the poem promises to hold together when it's all done, and then breaks off because life itself remains unfinished.

Among the better multi-part, chapbook-length poems are several attempts at a discursive ars poetica. *A Theory of Poetry* (1977) promises, and often delivers, serious advice:

> discover
> particular people at a particular time
> & in a particular place
> these people are the others
> without whom you would not exist . . .
>
> useful activities include
> eating talking & dancing
> listening to music (preferably live bands
> looking at paintings & undressing
> dressing & undressing

"A Theory of Poetry" also promises (perhaps self-mockingly) to "subvert any / deny any / positive / negative / narrative reading / & stress the written surface / with all its openings windows apertures leaks". Such writing invites us to embrace uncritically its resistance to "official verse culture", or else to give up on it as mostly unmade, as hops and barley rather than beer. Both responses ought to be resisted; the poems are good enough to invite real attention, and real distinctions between more and less accomplished work. James' consistent weaknesses are disorganization, garrulity, and a willingness to settle for in-jokes or mere records of experience: his strengths are spontaneity, vivid responsiveness, and a sense that in his poetry (even more than in real life) absolutely anything could come next. James' most achieved single works include "Poem of Inevitable September", "Side Window", "A Public Self-Address System", "Craven Images" part 1, "Bad Thoughts", "John Wilkinson's photo", "After Christopher Wood", "Sister Midnight", "For the Safety of Lovers", "Nijinsky", "From the Welsh", and "Idyl". He needs, now, a small, portable, *Selected*, one in which his casualness would not be permitted to wear out its welcome – a volume, in fact, like O'Hara's slim *Lunch Poems*, fans of which should certainly give James a listen.

Visiting Shadows

JAN MONTEFIORE

Elaine Feinstein, *Collected Poems and Translations*
Carcanet, £14.95 ISBN 1857545664

THE POINT OF a *Collected Poems* is to bring together at an affordable price a lifetime's intelligent dedication to the art of poetry, which this impressive collection does admirably – though if the intention of this book is to introduce Elaine Feinstein to new readers, a smaller selection might have done the job better. Feinstein is a respected poet who feels herself to be an outsider. Her sense of being on the periphery is made plain in a sharply intelligent poem "Annus Mirabilis 1989":

Ten years ago, beneath the Hotel Astoria,
   we watched a dissident cabaret in Budapest,
where they showed Einstein as a Jewish tailor.
   All the women on stage were elegantly dressed.

Their silken garments were cleverly slit to expose
   illicit glimpses of delicate thigh and breast.
Einstein was covered with chalk, in ill-fitting clothes;
   he was taking measurements, trying to please the rest.

At the climax of the play, to applause and laughter
   they raked him with strobe lights and the noise of guns.
I was chilled by the audience euphoria.
   Of course, I don't have a word of Hungarian,

And afterwards there were embarrassed explanations,
   which left out tailoring and obsequious gestures.
Their indignation was all about nuclear science, while
   I pondered the resilience of an old monster.

As a Jewish woman who remembers being offered the spectacle of delicious female bodies served up to the audience's pleasure, and of a vicious anti-Semitic staged fantasy of ritual humiliation and murder, Feinstein looks quizzically at the euphoria with which the West greeted the "velvet revolution" of Eastern European dissidents. Sliding between the rich formality of "illicit glimpses of delicate thigh and breast" and the conversational ease of "Of course, I don't have a word of Hungarian", her irony leaves her, as Virginia Woolf said of women, "on the outside, alien and critical".

Feinstein is not a poet who identifies herself with a "we"; even when writing of her Jewishness or her family, she emphasises separation and difference. Her closest affinity with other women poets is with the Russian poets she has translated with such skill and sensitivity, notably Marina Tsvetayeva and Bella Akhmadulina, who are much aware of the tensions existing between their lives as poets and as lovers, wives and mothers, and who made that tension the subject of much of their poetry. Her translations have a passionate directness that she doesn't often allow herself when writing in her own person: Tsvetayeva's defiant "We shall not escape Hell, my passionate sisters", celebrating and mourning those who "dressed every morning in / fine Chinese silk . . . slovenly needlewomen (all / our sewing came apart), dancers / players upon pipes: we have been / the queens of the whole world!"; Bella Akhamdulina's "Fever", that mixed blessing of poetic vocation –

      no ordinary illness. I'm sorry to
   tell you, there are as many wild and
   alien creatures flashing about in me
   as in a drop of water under a microscope.

Feinstein's awareness of the difficulty and exhilaration of being a woman poet might look feminist. Certainly some of the themes and approaches of her work, notably the long sequence-poems of classical mythology seen from the woman's point of view (Melusine in "The Celebrants", the "New Songs for Dido and Aeneas" and the "Songs for Eurydice") have much in common with the 1980s feminist project celebrated by Alicia Ostriker in "The Thieves of Language", of reclaiming the world of myth for women writers. In the poems of passion and awkwardness addressed to her husband, the sense of her own difference and longing "to make peace with her own monstrous nature", her sense of the tragedies of history, of coming from a victimised people, and of her difference and apartness as a woman, she has something in common with the Irish poet Eavan Boland. But making the comparison immediately points up a difference, for, unlike Boland, she has not constructed a poetic rhetoric or invoked an imagined community out of her own sense of being "outside history". Isobel Armstrong has noted that in some contemporary women poets "self-conscious concern with the multiple forms of language arises from a need not to be trapped inside the expressive self of the female subject, but the obligation, as a female subject, to release the lyric 'I' from the trap of a narrow identity politics . . . [and] to adopt multiple identities and selfhoods, and many voices and registers, in the effort to escape from a single national identity, become stateless, even alien, in order to record a history of oppression". This fits Elaine Feinstein's poetry closely, even though – but also, in a sense, because – it comes in a book (*Contemporary Women Poets*, eds. Alison Mark and Deryn Rees-Jones, 2000) in which Feinstein's name does not appear.

Much stronger than a sense of identification with any group is the sad yet sometimes joyful sense of impermanence which can be seen in "Night Thoughts" where the poet contemplates her own reflection in a dark kitchen window:

> My shelves of orange skillets
>   lie out in the black grass.
> Tonight I can almost taste
>   the wet soil of their ghosts.
> And my spirit looks through the glass:
>   I cannot hold on for ever.
>
> No tenure, in garden trees I
>   hang like a leaf, and stare
> at cartilaginous shapes
>   my shadow their visitor.
> And words cannot brazen it out:
>   Nothing can hold for ever.

Certainly the pots and pans represent the poet's life as a woman preserving and maintaining life in a human house; but the garden in the rain and the Le Creuset casseroles aren't part of any feminist domestic pastoral, as in Eavan Boland or Gillian Clarke: they are just the milieu and the tools for living that the poet happens to inhabit and use for a brief moment of her life – and already they are ghostly.

Very many of Feinstein's poems are elegies; she writes poignantly about the famous and the obscure, Joseph Brodsky, the no-hoper "Jimmy, nabbed again at the Elephant", and most touchingly her father ("Your old hat hurts me, and those black / fat raisins you liked to press into / my palm from your soft heavy hand"). Even poems that are not explicitly elegiac tend to memorialise happiness as the briefest of moments, as in "Coastline" where in "a landscape of the Cambrian age . . . iron and lead; soapstone, spars of calcite . . . fish . . . the colour of sand, / velvet crabs like weeds, prawns transparent as water", her two young sons are seen "bent-backed, intent" on their fishing while "further out, Time and Chance are waiting to happen". Seen in the inhumanly long perspective of geological time, this moment of family happiness has an ironic pathos. So do the mortal bodies contemplated in "The Celebrants":

> And this knowledge enters even
>   between the bodies of lovers, though
> we share each other's vigil; that our arms
>
> hold water only, salt as the sea
>   we come from, a spongework of
> acid chains, our innermost landscape
>
>   an arcane pulp of flexible
>   chemistry: sinus, tubes,
>   follicles, cells that wander

The last of these stanzas keeps too close to the biology textbook, not quite living up to the wit and plangent bleakness of "our arms / hold water only". But, like all her poems, it is never less than intelligent, sharply phrased, and deeply felt.

The Escapade Goat

ANDREW DUNCAN

Robert Fraser, *Chameleon Poet. The Life of George Barker*
Jonathan Cape, £25, ISBN 0224062425

MUCH HAS BEEN written, since 1957, about the "mid-century death" in English poetry. It does not apply to George Barker (1913–91). The son of a housemaid and an unemployed ex-soldier (later a servant at Gray's Inn), a poet without secondary education, Barker was really a different kind of person from his poetic rivals (and reviewers). He wrote passionate, highly organised, linguistically gorgeous, personally charged poetry, partly because he was too ignorant to know that this wouldn't go down well with reviewers:

> The colossal Apollo. The sky-writer with
> Guilt in his thumbmark, the poet with the human
> Hanging at hand, cut with a verb to the nerve,
> Rabbits at butchers. The arrogant wreath
> Bright at his face, the Mephisphelean omen,
> Both wards away and draws a man and woman.
> O seeking at all altars a Sibylline to serve
> Either in beds or wars, he finds only
> The anthropoid I gibbering from mirrors. Lonely
> The poet walks among a score of selves.
>
> (from "Eros in Dogma")

His power relies on a triangle of excitement: the emoting person in the poem, the poet, and the reader. His reconstruction of unstable states is robust. We want to be the third point of the triangle.

Although Robert Fraser, author of *Chameleon Poet: The life of George Barker*, basically cannot write literary criticism, his laborious working out of Barker's family predicaments at datable moments amounts to necessary reading for anyone who now wishes to study Barker's poetry at length. Barker wrote far too much, but then Fraser did a terrific *Selected Poems* a few years ago. You really should read *The True Confession of George Barker*, *Calamiterror*, and *The Seraphina*, if only to make your mind up.

Barker fitted into English literary life like an Irish barmaid at a Methodist picnic. He was, simply, a Methodist's nightmare of a working-class Catholic – feckless, fertile, verbal, virile. Barker had fifteen children. This did not happen without women saying yes from time to time, and to a certain extent this prohibits us from saying no. As usual with philanderers, you get the impression sometimes that the women made the key decisions, that he was weak, that deception was by consent, that he flowed into the preset images of their desires. He conformed – it's just that it wasn't male authority he conformed to. Logically, the story of Barker's life is much more about the romantic conceptions of mid-century women than it is about Barker himself – and from this perspective, his poetry is an endless chat-up line, the soundtrack to a steamy, swooning, novelette. Fraser's biography fails because it doesn't read like a woman's picture of the 1940s ("extensive suffering in expensive clothes", etc.). Barker was tall, dark, sinewy, saturnine, volatile, striking-looking, acknowledged no masters, had an air of secret suffering, a way with words, a chequered past, he was available – well, at five minutes' notice, really. Did it take a feather to knock them down? Who was the cat, who the mouse? He made promises to one woman which he kept with several others. There is no record of women asking for chastity from Barker – you could say, they got what they wanted. Betty Cass spent many hours listening to Barker agonizing about strains between his wife and the mother of most of his children, and then began an affair with him. Christ! What an idiot! But someone describes her as "Dior's ambassador to the Communist Party", and we realise that what the book needs is more clothes. Much more about clothes. More sex. More cross-class sex. More raffish Soho anecdotes.

James Keery has written an as yet unpublished essay in which he points out that there was no difference between the Apocalyptics and the New Romantics – they were the same people. Fraser says that Barker belonged to the latter but indignantly denies that he was part of the former. What do we find? He was obsessed with visceral symbolism, believed in the reality of human desires over social institutions, did not believe in the "object-machine", believed in his own prophetic insight, constantly used imagery from myth, claimed to interpret contemporary history and once wrote "I am John of Patmos", was weak at reasoning – how could he *not* be Apocalyptic? As Keery says, the distinction into two groups is *ex post facto*, an act of hostility, and does not hold water. The biographical approach shoves style history into a darkened quadrant.

Barker went to a psychiatrist, who diagnosed "religious mania" and prescribed methedrine as a cure for it. Barker acquired a meth habit, and "had also become dependent on benzedrine, hacked from the linings of cigarette lighters with a penknife and then dunked in tea". Gascoyne, Graham, Auden, now Barker – English poetry at that time had a jet intake up its nose. Barker was a Catholic who ignored the structures of the Church, had no spiritual adviser, distrusted the organisation, rejected the Magisterium, saw holiness in sexual congress and in secular life, and sought to make up his own mind according to a private revelation – in other words, he was a Protestant.

While Fraser says that Barker's emotion and lack of education were the brave opening of a new era, I disagree. The story is, rather, a wonderful advance into the world of ideas, as the intelligent gradually recovered from a panic about intelligence. Barker is no less marginal now than in 1930. Whether you like or dislike his poetry probably depends on your feelings about being plunged into someone else's sex melodrama. Eliot said (of the two novellas in *Janus*) "They will give pleasure to readers who are civilized enough to be primitive and honest enough to recognize their own feelings". It does seem that Barker was Eliot's artistic *paredros*, the double who led the bold life (artistically and personally). While Eliot wrote conservatively and took care of business, Barker was the escapade goat.

Because Barker systematically misled everyone and did not keep documentation, producing a connected biography was clearly a major effort, demanding luck, great personal charm, and years of diligence. Biographers use consistency as a test of their material. But Barker was completely inconsistent, as Fraser keeps telling us. There is therefore no strong reason for accepting the coherent picture this biography draws. When writing introspectively, Barker could only come up with deviousness and distraction – the *Confession* starts in overdrive, stays in overdrive, but lacks forward motion and design. Barker was not a poet who believed in the self as a body of retrievable and connected knowledge: the self as a filing cabinet that contains the poem. Barker's poetic vitality makes most of his rivals look quite ridiculous. The lesson is that poets shouldn't spend their time reading long boring prose books – like this one.

In 1948, Barker published a brutal review of Dunstan Thompson. Fraser misinterprets this whole incident. The hostility arose from the fact that Thompson was an imitator of Barker, equally indebted to Hopkins or Francis Thompson, and equally "Catholic Baroque". "American poetry", Barker wrote, "is a very simple subject to discuss for the simple reason that it does not exist." In 1946–7? Come off it! Barker rejected education because he didn't want objectivity – when he argues, it feels like having your head banged against a brick wall. Thompson's obvious feyness problematically reframed Barker's flamboyance. Perhaps the baroque theatrical style of both poets could be redefined by administrative experts on maleness as being shrill and exaggerated. I decline this expertise. I no more believe that Thompson's theatricality is shallow than I believe that ornate speech is a breach of the Act of Uniformity.

Barker is generally described as Baroque. His work often relies on memories of Italian Baroque works of art – his primary school was the London Oratory. The favoured field of the academic New Critics who shunned him was the Metaphysicals – who, in any other language, would be called Baroque. Donne was indebted to Spanish and Italian poetry. So why is there so much dissension here? Hill, the major heir of the Metaphysical influence, is also Barker's heir – *The Triumph of Love* and *Speech! Speech!* are closer to long Barker poems like *Anno Domini*, *In Memoriam David Archer*, and the *True Confession*, than to anything else.

His Own Unhappy Knack

MICHAEL GRANT

Donald Davie, *Collected Poems,* edited by Neil Powell
Carcanet, £14.95, ISBN 1857544064

IN AN ESSAY of 1959 (reprinted in *The Poet in the Imaginary Museum*), Donald Davie presented himself, and those contemporaries associated with him in the Movement, in a light at once harsh and unforgiving. What underpinned his remarkably brutal self-exposure was the question of tone. The thing that stuck in his craw was what he came to see as the peculiarly deprecating and ingratiating tone of voice in which the poetry of the group had presented itself to the educated readers of its time. As Davie icily remarks, what, in effect, the poets of the Movement had succeeded in doing was to replace a poetry of self-expression (the poetry of Dylan Thomas and Edith Sitwell) with one no less egregious, namely, a poetry of "self-adjustment" – a poetry dedicated to getting on the right terms with the reader and to hitting off the right attitude towards him or her. Davie came to see the poetry he had written during the 1950s as an act of public and private therapy, in its own way another and no less contemptible mode of self-expression. His work, and that of those associated with him, was guilty of what during the 1960s and onwards he was to regard as *the* cardinal sin: the failure to respond creatively to the world as such. For the English poets of the 1950s, he believed, the world out there, in its quiddity, was accessible, if at all, only by way of an overweening irony, at once self-defensive and self-deprecating, which denied the world its integrity and otherness. Things in themselves were permitted no impact upon the poet unless submitted to categories and attitudes he or she had already imposed upon them. As Davie puts it: "This imperiousness towards the non-human goes along with excessive humility towards the human, represented by the reader." To make the manipulation of "tone" the central preoccupation of poetry was to deny the ontological in the interests of the social. The refusal, characteristic of English poetry from Yeats, Auden, and Empson to the Movement, and on to Thom Gunn and others, to accept the reality of "alien modes of being" was taken by Davie to be symptomatic of a deeper malaise: the catastrophic failure to acknowledge the reality of being as such. Awareness of this failure was to remain for Davie, throughout his life, a touchstone of what he saw as the peculiar deadness lying at the heart of English culture and mentality. Davie noted it especially in the willingness of modern English poets (including Hardy) to sell poetry short, and in the diminished expectations and philistinism of the culture as a whole.

What Davie's *Collected Poems* reveal is a constant struggle to overcome these failures, as he saw them, within himself.

> Worry hedges my days
> Like a roil of thick mist at the edge of a covert
> Fringing a tufted meadow. In that field
> Monuments of art and sanctity
> Arise in turn before
> The clouded glass of my eye.
> Last year two churches of St Francis
> Were piled up there, at the lowest verge of Assisi.

This poem, "On Not Deserving", from *Poems of 1962–1963*, is suggestive in its ambiguities. There is in place a "roil" of thick mist obscuring the edge of a covert which is compared to the "worry" hedging the poet's days. The first line implies that worry not only limits or sets bounds to the speaker's days, it also allows him to hedge his bets and to trim, to hold to the middle course and avoid extremes. "Roil", which as a verb means to rile, vex, or annoy, or to make water muddy or unclear by stirring, has become a substantive, a displacement of use which effects precisely the blurring of boundaries essential to the poet's strategy here. Furthermore, the boundary or edge in question is the edge of a covert, itself a hiding-place, a thicket hiding game. The field thus delimited by the poem is of uncertain definition. However, it is here that "Monuments of art and sanctity", invoking the transcendence of Yeats's "Monuments of unageing intellect" and the humility of St Francis, are said to "arise", and "arise in turn". "Turn" evokes "verse", and "before" points to what comes next, which is, as we pull over the line end, "The clouded glass of my eye". Here, the poem is showing itself for what it is, a "turn" – a turn that clarifies what it clarifies with respect to an eye whose glass is "clouded". To clarify is thus an obscuring. The opacity of the situation is marked in the last line by the spatial deictic "there", suspended before the caesura and pointing back to the equally unfocussed temporal marker of the previous line – "Last year". Just as the poem seems poised to impose its images on the world, so, in the same gesture, the flat, almost paratactic phrasing seems on the "verge" of withdrawing them, as too overweening an importunity. What is piled up is piled up at "the lowest verge of Assisi", a phrase that fails to point to anything, except perhaps itself, engaged in the act of pointing. The speaker is not "deserving", not worthy – of what, we don't know – on the evidence of the very act he has just performed. He has accomplished his own failure, and, as it were, by pleading his innocence established his guilt. The poem's lack is the possibility of its being.

"The Hill Field" (*Events and Wisdoms*, 1964) is a more extended and complex piece in the same vein:

Look here! What a wheaten
Half-loaf, halfway to bread,
A cornfield is, that is eaten
Away, and harvested.

How like a loaf, where the knife
Has cut and come again,
Jagged where the farmer's wife
Has served the farmer's men,

That steep field is, where the reaping
Has only just begun
On a wedge-shaped front, and the creeping
Steel edges glint in the sun.

See the cheese-like shape it is taking,
The sliced-off walls of the wheat
And the cheese-mite reapers making
Inroads there, in the heat?

It is Brueghel or Samuel Palmer,
Some painter, coming between
My eye and the truth of a farmer,
So massively sculpts the scene.

The sickles of poets dazzle
These eyes that were filmed from birth;
And the miller comes with an easel
To grind the fruits of earth.

This poem, like the first I quoted, refers to other writing. The reference here is to "The Solitary Reaper". The poem also refers to itself, as the singular act of composition that it is. That is, in referring to itself, it simultaneously refers us to another writing. This is to stress, not intertextual reference in general, but rather the singularity of the act of referral itself. What Davie has here constructed is a poem that is open and closed at once. Because of the uncertainty of context which this play of reference creates, an uncertainty concerning who is saying what to whom, the poem's tone – its explicit "address" to the reader – can no longer be understood as it was by Davie in 1959. That this is so can be seen at the beginning of the opening line. The imperative, "Look here", serves to confirm the identity of *this* text (or, at any rate, of *this* phrase) by moving outside or beyond itself, in order to point to itself from the position of an other, the reader who is addressed by words that apparently refer only to the event of the poem itself – the event of the poem's *depicting* what is depicted by it. (This "event", it would seem, is the poem's "wisdom".) The phrase, "Look here", can of course also be read as an expostulation. The status of the poem's beginning is thus rendered immediately problematic.

This point may be made clearer with respect to the image of the field which is in play here, as in "On Not Deserving", and which fulfils much the same role in this poem as it did in that. The image of the field is what the poem is in the process of constructing, and part of what the image is an image of is the process whereby it is being constructed. In effect, what the poem shows is itself as it emerges from, or is engendered by, the process of being said. As a critic, Davie had elaborated on this kind of symbolist configuration in essays on Eliot, Pound, Mallarmé, and Pasternak, some of which were written prior to or during the composition of the poetry of this collection. Thus, in "The Hill Field", as with many other poems he wrote during the same period, one can see the poet developing a complex modernist poetry based on that of the earlier masters, but as it were transposed into what looks like the minor key of a poet who also has his eye on Hardy, a poet who was, according to Davie, unlike Eliot and the other major modernists in that he failed to transform or displace "quantifiable reality or the reality of common sense". In "The Hill Field", symbolist techniques are present, and signalled as such. "Wheaten" is reduced to "eaten" as the "half-loaf" of the field set up by the poem is reduced by the removal, or harvesting, of the letters "wh". In stanza three, "the wedge-shaped front" is there on the page, shown in the shape constructed by the way the words "and creeping" in line 3 protrude beyond the second and fourth lines. The apostrophe "how", beginning at line 5, is only revealed to be an apostrophe, rather than a question, by the end of line 12. The opening "See" of line 13 looks like another apostrophe, but by the end of line 16 it is seen in retrospect to be a question. The palpability of the words is further emphasised by sound: "ee" provides a kind of basic pattern, through which other vowels intertwine in a series of complex variations.

More generally, the poem doubles back on itself, as though it were referring to itself referring to itself. It separates itself from itself and by so doing opens a gap within its structure across which reference can operate. This is signalled and effected by the temporal displacement at the opening, whereby the cornfield is presented as already the loaf it has not yet become, a loaf baked before the harvest is gathered in. It is in this temporal shifting that we see what gives rise to the various metaphors of violation carried by words like "knife", "cut", "cheese-mites", and the "sickles" (inevitably evoking "versicles") that occur throughout the text. By means of a folding or turning back of time on itself, something that occurs only in the order of writing, the end is enabled to precede the beginning, and the beginning to come after the end. The device results in so profound a rupturing or undoing of intelligible order that, as Davie describes it, in an essay on syntax and music, there remains to the reader only one order of time which he can trust: "the one time the tale takes in the telling, the time which the poem takes to be spoken or read". This foregrounding of the device, or *ostranenie*, is a procedure central to the poetry of Pasternak, as Davie's essays and book on him make abundantly clear, and it is central also to his own:

> Most poems, or the best,
> Describe their own birth, and this
> Is what they are – a space
> Cleared to walk around in.
>
> ("Ars Poetica")

The ramifications of this reach very far. A word that has special privilege in Davie's earlier poetry is "edge", and there are others related to it, like "knife", cut", "sculpture", "stone", and words and names associated with art more generally. "Edge" seems to have the same role here as "blanc" in Mallarmé. Like Mallarmé's writing (or Pasternak's), Davie's is a writing of *spacing* – in the sense that it foregrounds spatio-temporal differing – and words like "edge" or "cut" or their substitutes refer to the very spaces or cuts that make possible the series of which they are themselves members. The edge thus understood is what gives to the poem the conditions both of the possibility of meaning and of its impossibility. Thus, in "The Hill Field", the names of the artists, Brueghel and Samuel Palmer, constitute a movement of undecidability: they mark what makes the poem possible and what stands outside, or transcends, that possibility, inasmuch as they mark what conditions it, "coming between / My eye and the truth of a farmer". The final stanza takes this further: in acknowledging that the poet's eyes were "filmed from birth", a play is engendered on "from" (inasmuch as "from" may mean both "since" and "due to") that is repeated in the double genitive in the last line: "fruits of earth" allows or constitutes a doubling which in turn allows (or calls forth) a play on "earth" itself, a word resonant with implication and connotation. The complex play of meaning and counter-meaning at the end of the poem is thus shown to be an effect internal to the conditions of writing as such. For an instance of a poem that can be said to take this procedure to the limit, see the extraordinary "Bolyai, the Geometer": it is a fully achieved symbolist poem in the mode of Pasternak.

And it is this excess, the excess of syntax over semantics, that Davie's work continued to explore, throughout *Events and Wisdoms* and beyond. To align Davie in this way with an advanced modernism, may seem, despite Davie's own critical clarification of these very modes of writing, perverse, wrong-headed. And yet, in "Sonnet", a poem of the 1980s, Davie writes: "the scarp / Of language you would quarry, poet, whirls / Indeterminately shaped in / Helix on nebulous helix, not to be netted". In "Thomas and Emma", which, according to the editor, Neil Powell, is the last poem Davie wrote, in July 1995, two months before his death, we read: "Hyperbole, analogy, allusion / Build up what is no lie, although so wishful: / Conspiratorial, conjugal collusion". The alliterations hark back to what "builds them up" and suggest that the "collusion", which is no lie, depends upon a poetic understanding of language that is hyperbolic, dependent upon analogy and allusive. I am not offering a modish characterisation or deconstruction of texts against the grain of an author who would have been resistant to readings of this kind. I am attempting rather to point to ways in which Davie came to see how the foundation of meaning in what is itself without meaning was inseparable from the vision his poetry gives us of what poetry, and so life, can or might be. It is here that his earlier self-castigation finds itself assuaged. In the enhanced sense his poetry shows of terms such as "between", "before", "after", and so on, terms which resist being straightforwardly conceptualised or being turned into nouns, as well as in its sensitivity to the syntactic exploitation of the different values of words, a thematic or moral reading of the texts must give way to something else – something more "nebulous", "not be netted".

> Moreover, space is encoded
> to signify lapses of time.
> (One verse-line under another;
> this one after that one.)

> The nearness of God is known as
> an aching absence:
> the room the reception-desk
> cannot locate nor account for,

in a fictitious or
analogous space that does not
answer to or observe
the parameters of Newton,

any more than a page of verse does.

This, from a late poem, "Thou Art Near At Hand, O Lord", is not an attempt to identify the language of modern poetry, with its predilection for negativity and a dialectic of lack, with that of negative theology. The lines serve only to suggest that the thematic or didactic, often seen as typical features of Davie's poetry, may not be as easy to identify there as we might like to think. The play of wit and irony, the play, that is, of the sudden idea and its ironic realisation or separation out into paradox, allows Davie a writing at once playful and serious. Davie's poetry is one of an interminable oscillation between meaning and the loss of it, between rapidity and the discursive. In this, Davie, the exponent of late Augustan order, is also the exponent of the romantic fragment, in which both creation and destruction are sustained. "He branches out, but only to collapse, / Imprisoned in his own unhappy knack, / Which, when unfailing, fails him most, perhaps". Perhaps, for Davie, the truth of literature is captured in that "perhaps".

With Surprising Affection

TONY LOPEZ

Ed Barrett, *Sheepshead Bay*
Zoland Books, $13, ISBN 1581951035

WASN'T THERE A Ted Berrigan poem that was a dream invoking Frank O'Hara coming back from death to talk to Ted – and wasn't that poem a version of O'Hara's "A True Account of Talking to the Sun at Fire Island"? If not there ought to have been. In Ed Barrett's poem "A Vision of Ted Berrigan in Cambridge, Massachusetts", Ted Berrigan comically doesn't want to talk about Barrett's poetry but sends him back from the dream vision with a message, a scene of harm and recovery: a clairvoyant scenario or maybe just a memory. Barrett seems to come back more aware of life and love as it is, present and miraculous.

All of this is stock we are used to and, for that reason perhaps, it is affecting if we are open to it. The world described in this wonderful collection of poems is a particular group of friends, artists and poets, connected with the New York School and their Boston associates. Poems are dedicated to John Ashbery, Bill Corbett, Trevor Winkfield, John Wieners, Charles North, Joe Brainard, Kenward Elmslie, and Ann Lauterbach (among others) and we have the sense that is there in O'Hara's and Berrigan's work of a coterie, of a scene becoming visible to itself in print. Barrett uses a wide range of compositional methods deliberately to push his writing further and to mix up a sometimes radical invention with what seems to be most deeply felt and personal. He plays with narrative possibilities that look like random generative permutations woven back in on themselves, not quite arbitrary but not fully explained.

I particularly liked "The Sonneteer" which turns out to be the name of a software package, a kind of love poem displaced by its own rhetorical profusion, trying to find a way to reach through absence and loss:

> I have surveilled this region day and night and still no trace of you. I must
> have been crazy buying reconnaissance software called *The Sonneteer*
> ("Because Life Is A Lesson In Grammar, A Series Of Endings!" "Direct
> Matters With Surprising Affection, Almost A Kind Of Knowledge About Life
> and Death, Dreaded As Thou Art!"). It offered to reach into the cone-shaped
> throat of darkness with my voice as through the surface of an icy stream, like a
> child trying to get at a shiny stone.

The lightest comic touch directs us through the special rhetoric of a software life-coaching
package to the primers of Renaissance courtly speech, and the heartbreak jokes ("a series of
endings", "dreaded as thou art") work both in the electronic and the historical era.

> Virgil held a blood-filled syringe and sang in perfect epic feet, *You'll never
> know if you don't know now*, and his words fell short of the kind of beautiful
> grouting work he is justly famous for, but they had an idle menacing beauty.
> And I remember the fear I felt, small and leafy, as once when I was a boy I
> rowed at low tide into the mouth of a storm drain at the end of Sheepshead
> Bay careful not to scrape against the walls and roof. The Virgin Mary held the
> mouth of the storm drain open for a minute while I let myself out.

("Tir na nOg")

Here we can recognise and appreciate the working out of purely formal associations of small and large containers filling with liquid and flushing, the generative acoustic similarity of Virgil and Virgin, and the particularly vivid experience of the fearful storm drain "one more thing floating in a world of shit". The deft humour is there again in "grouting work" and "small and leafy".

Gothic touches renovate an old-fashioned and developing sense (across several poems) of a Catholic boyhood, growing up in Brooklyn. "By No Stretch of the Imagination" is a poem that takes literally and tries on as a title a clichéd phrase that might have been Romantic usage had we seen its potential. The poem is a parody of self-aware writing, at times apparently a meditation on what people mean when they ask you about writing, imaging the poet as a mutant person with the writing organs displayed on the surface, gills on the side

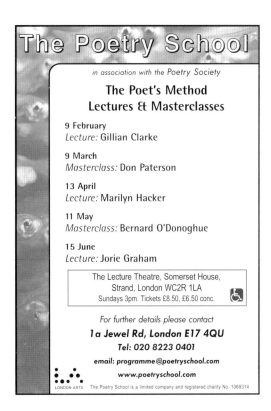

of the poet's face. I can't respond fully to such a piece without re-iterating the narrative particulars of the poem in their surreal conjunctions but the link between these two, "By No Stretch of the Imagination" and "Tir na nOg", is telling. Both of them mention the Sheepshead Bay of the book title, and both evoke touching memories of childhood love and loss among the flashy narrative profusion: "I am lonely for Sheepshead Bay and my father and the boat we had". The very simplicity and directness of this has a quality and power derived from the complexity in which it is embedded.

"Intimations of Immortality" (dedicated to Charles North) is an imaginary awards ceremony with nominations in such categories as "Best Sandwich", "Best Food Additive", "Best Way to Die", "Best Excuse". The main body of the poem is in each case a list of nominations, followed by a section of winners and a guest list that reads like the late arrivals item on "I'm Sorry I Haven't A Clue". The winning sandwich is BLT. Yes, this is like one of Berrigan's 1960s list poems such as "The Ten Greatest Books of the Year, 1968" or "People Who Died" (a good poem showing just the same ambition to use ludicrous means to get through afresh to the experience of loss). But it would be wrong to overplay the comparison with Berrigan and to claim that this sumptuous and original poetry was a retro-art in thrall to a vanished 1960s American writing. It is made just as much from the unresolvable narrative impulses of John Ashbery, the playfully deliberate working out of elaborate conceits by Kenneth Koch, and the ornate visual exuberance of Trevor Winkfield. What distinguishes Ed Barrett's poetry is the fluency with which re-workings of traditional poetic ideas are tied to the speed and rapid scale shifting of the computer game. I liked "The Lighthouse Family" and "Pilgrims Undaunted by Speed" for their absolutely contemporary use of popular culture, science and non-religious transcendence:

> Is it not possible, asks the engineering genius, that someday the path may be established more directly? But the world as meditation ravels and unravels its sailors in black watch caps and bell bottoms, moves rubies round from jeweler to skin conditions in a very prodigal manner. Who are you to think like a beacon piercing the ocean of night like that? And what do you get out of it?
>
> ("The Lighthouse Family")

> I go to MIT too, in a way, so I curled my index finger down into the space between it and my thumb to make a perfectly round pin-hole and modeled my version of the eclipse on the sidewalk in front of me, held literally in the palm of my hand the mystery of darkness in its flight across our day.
>
> ("Pilgrims Undaunted by Speed")

Like the best of Barrett's poems these pieces are written in fluent detailed prose that finds its imaginative energy in poetic conceits: in taking the name of a pop group literally, in judging the best sandwich, in personalising the experience of a heavenly eclipse, in turning rhetoric and proving the world miraculous. It is 5:15am in Exmouth, the 15th of July.

The Middle Distance

ANDREA BRADY

Lorine Niedecker, *Collected Works*, edited by Jenny Penberthy
University of California Press, £29.95, ISBN 0520224337

> I was the solitary plover
> a pencil
> for a wing-bone

THE PENCIL'S LEAD core plugging hollow bone: through this image of solitude and the desire for flight, as throughout Lorine Niedecker's poetry, there runs a vein of self-assurance so forceful and complete it exceeds even the dramatics of performed and public resistance. This excerpt from "Paean to Place" may at first suggest the cultural myth of the isolated and fragile female writer; but it's a myth, as Adrienne Rich points out, that doesn't particularly suit Lorine Niedecker. Among the varieties of plover, a bird which doesn't migrate in winter from its lakeside habitats, is the killdeer, *Charadrius vociferus*, which pretends to have broken a wing when an enemy gets too close to its nest. Breakage that distracts attention to another site, and allows the animal to elude its pursuers, is perhaps a more appropriate emblem for Niedecker's unique and challenging work.

Although she spent much of her life in comparative isolation by the lakes of Wisconsin, a location whose significance to her poetry she recognised in the title of her last book *My Life by Water* (1970), Niedecker lived in the American middle distance. Eking out a living in that overlooked space between the economic, political, and cultural capitals of both coasts, she too was often overlooked by publishers, despite the real originality of her poetry, despite even the relationships she built from a lifetime of intelligent, self-deprecating correspondence. It has consequently been difficult to get hold of her work – a difficulty now relieved by the *Collected Works*, edited by Jenny Penberthy and newly published by the University of California Press.

Niedecker lived very much in the middle of things, both natural and social, moving from the flowers and creatures of her own acutely observed, accurately named biosphere, to the effects of war, capital, poverty, and gender relations which impacted on it. Her solitude was peopled with the neighbours and family whose own lyrical and idiomatic speech she transcribes directly, for example, in "The museum man!". Her reading extended away from these localities, to European philosophical and literary traditions; her poems seem both spontaneous and researched, fastening on neighbourhood dynamics at the same time as they contemplate the metaphysical consequences of Einstein's theories.

Born in 1903, Niedecker grew up in Fort Atkinson, Wisconsin, and briefly attended Beloit College. After her marriage began and ended in two Depression-era years, she moved back to her parents' home to care for her deaf mother. In 1938, Niedecker began working for one of Roosevelt's economic development engines, the Works Project Administration, as a writer and research editor. Some of her best poems date from this period, when out of her consideration of local language and habitat for the guides to Wisconsin she was writing, emerged the folk cadences of her best-known book, *New Goose*. Later, when failing eyesight forced her to give up her next job as a stenographer, Niedecker experienced severe financial hardship which increasingly denied her the time to write.

From 1957 to 1963, she worked as a cleaner in a hospital, until a second marriage removed her to Milwaukee and allowed her to return full-time to writing. She died in 1970. Throughout a life of labour, floods and fluctuations, she practiced the one trade from which there would be "No layoff": "condensery".

Her earliest poems demonstrate a home-grown Surrealist imagination, even before Louis Zukofsky referred her to *transition* magazine "for correlation". Occasionally overwrought, these poems show the earliest formation of what seem to me most characteristic of Niedecker's mesmeric poetry: the simple diction made peculiar through place, the deceptively simple rhythms gathering pace through lengthy periods punctuated also by a fine sensitivity to prosody:

> This swale
> can only be the mode by which we condense all exposition
> to a green blood-beat and bleach intact. Let no man say
> from grass to grass he never to himself has sunk
> is the first tremble of an old vibration orioled
> at dandelion heat. In Swalery I forget my face,
> beyond that it's something to have under a sunbonnet
> when aphorists and haymakers meet.

After reading the Objectivist number of *Poetry* magazine (February 1931), Niedecker began a weekly correspondence with Zukofsky, and her poems begin to demonstrate the clarity and sincerity associated with that ad hoc movement. Later, she also corresponded regularly with Cid Corman, Kenneth Cox, Bob Nero, and Clayton Eshleman, and became acquainted with, and admired by, poets including Ian Hamilton Finlay, Basil Bunting, Marianne Moore, and William Carlos Williams. Her difficulty in securing publication is part not only of her complicated relation – and often unwilling subsumption – to the Objectivist moniker, but also (as Peter Middleton has argued) her own determinedly local poetics. A fidelity to everyday speech and to the particulars of her natural and civic environments, along with her reluctance to perform her work publicly, situated Niedecker in a specific locality which itself became a vocation.

Jenny Penberthy's service to the reappraisal of Niedecker's poetry began with her *Lorine Niedecker: Woman and Poet*. As in her edition *Niedecker and the Correspondence with Zukofsky, 1931–1970*, the editorial work in this *Collected* is exacting. In addition to retrieving Niedecker's prose poems and radio plays, Penberthy reproduces each sequence and book in its entirety (even when that entails reprinting individual poems), ensuring the integrity of the sequences in all the phases of their development. Niedecker's poetry often depends on the return of a melodic burden, on the molting of particular phrases and dashes; the (occasionally distracting) reprinting points the reader's attention to these arcs, developments, and displacements. Penberthy's notes also supply detailed records of Niedecker's emendations and corrigienda. Just as she used the Zukofsky correspondence to "disengage Niedecker from the myth of Zukofsky", Penberthy shows a staunchness in resisting the revisions suggested by Zukofsky which is also one of the few conspicuously dogmatic instances in her editorship.

In her *Niedecker Correspondence*, Penberthy offers a psychological reading of Niedecker's notably intense dedication to Zukofsky's and Celia Thaew's son Paul. She contends that Niedecker had an abortion, at Zukofsky's insistence, after their brief affair in

1933. This claim, based somewhat tenuously on reports by Jerry Reisman and Mary Oppen, is not really pursued in her introduction to this *Collected Works*. To focus on it there or here risks attributing some element of Niedecker's creativity to psychological crises about reproduction. Nonetheless, it is true that in the poems *For Paul*, Niedecker transforms the anecdotes of his son's childhood which Zukofsky shared into a loving and imaginative attachment. It is perhaps in these poems, with their admiration for the cultured home where the baby violinist is growing up, that Niedecker comes closest to expressing a discontent with her own home, its limited cultural access and lack of like minds. More positively, *For Paul* also provides an opportunity to introduce the child to the world, mimicking phenomenal wonders with her own poetry's scrupulous strangeness and nursery rhythms.

Niedecker doesn't blanch, for example, from explaining war to the boy; and many of her reflections on war also imagine particularly the abandoned child, as in "Wartime" which begins:

> I left my baby in Forest A
> quivering toward light:
> Keep warm, dear thing, drink from the cow –
> her stillness is alive

There is an unsentimental bravery in Niedecker's use of the personal, although the personal can also become invisible without disappearing: the lack of pronominal referents in some later poems, or the reductive syntax which mystifies subjective experience as it renders it in apparently direct language, does not affirm a wholly materialist vision of a universe without ethics. Rather, Niedecker's poetry ratifies a kind of natural law, a set of compulsions derived by right-thinking observers from nature's own works. But if that is the code of her own ethics, Niedecker's pragmatism keeps watch dialectically over the discrepancies between natural law and human action: and especially over their alarming divergence during the mid-century.

Without being mystical, programmatic or in fact complex at the level of diction or syntax, Niedecker's work produces complicated effects. It teases out sonorities from the briefest phrases, pauses over visual rhymes, and seems regularly entranced with its own elliptical informalities. It is, moreover, conspicuously civic, rooted in the experience and politics of labour, in the community, and especially in the environment which not only provides a scenic and sonic background to that community's life, but shapes it as much as it shapes her poetry formally. Niedecker read Marx and Engels, and Zukofsky forwarded her his copies of radical magazines. Though never affiliated to any party, and subject to a decreasing political interest with age, Niedecker homes in on the strange and confusing world of war, fascism, post-war consumerism and the atom bomb, in such poems as "European Travel (Nazi New Order)" or "I am sick with the Time's buying sickness".

The localism of her political consciousness risks a certain sentimentality. She writes with sincerity and attention about individuals, but rarely so about classes or other collectives. For example: an early poem, "No retiring summer stroke", concludes

> not the pop play of tax, borrow or inflate
> but the radiant, tight energy
> boring from within

        communizing fear
        into strike,
        work.

Although the poem does not refer explicitly to the workers who may radiate that "tight energy" and open up power relations from within, it uses its own material and deperson-alised existence as a correlative for their forcefulness. In this way, it fulfils the intention she expressed in a letter to *Poetry* editor Harriet Monroe: "The effect of propaganda in poetic (?) form has the effect on me of swearing that I as a writer will portray my epoch and truthfully evoke life in its totalities only as I am able to make magic, magic of dream and deep subconscious and waking isolation thick unto impenetrability".

As her politics became less overt, and her fears of a technologically-driven post-war culture seemed to increase, her lyrics became increasingly and almost uselessly spare. They flatten at last into a rather artless simplicity, especially "Harpsichord and Salt Fish", a skeletal cousin to Williams's *In the American Grain*. With this text the pressure she brings to bear on locality collapses, I think, and the goal of "evoking life in its totalities" degenerates into a proud discovery of the particular in national identity.

Of course, the presence of such considerations differentiates Niedecker's condensery from the Imagism she rejected as a young writer. In one of her most powerfully feminist statements, "I rose from marsh mud", Niedecker commemorates a wedding of a "little white slave-girl / in her diamond fronds" to a husband who is not named. The ceremony concludes with the two "United for life to serve / silver. Possessed." The image embodies Niedecker's critique not only of the girl's domestic or sexual servitude, but also of the con-taminating economic utility of marriage. Likewise, her suggestions about gender are not attentive primarily to reproduction, but to political action and self-determination, as in "North Central", where women are early environmentalists:

        Who saved it?—
            Women
                        of good wild stock
        stood stolid
            before machines
                        They stopped bulldozers
        cold

But, with all her pride in the "social", the powers of the community to resist and to withstand suffering, Niedecker also confides a certain dread: in "In the great snowfall before the bomb", she writes:

        I worked the print shop
        right down among em
        the folk from whom all poetry flows
        and dreadfully much else.

Though she affirms their "vitality", she also regrets "their rehashed radio barbs", the prejudices of the folk which allowed the catastrophes of National Socialism to overwhelm Europe.

To be at the shoreline of the Wisconsin lakeland, in the middle of things, is also to be in a liminal space between land and water; between the high cultural nexus of her New York correspondents and the folk culture of her own acquaintances; between the deep fidelity to locality and the discomfiting alienation from a locality which is changing; between a solidarity in labour and a recognition of difference in her commitments to the unrecognised, unpaid labour of writing.

The disappointments, the solitude, the refusal to write happily about marriage, and especially the elliptical or truncated syntax, inevitably invite comparisons between Niedecker's poetry and that of Emily Dickinson. Readers and critics have probably had a bad conscience about Niedecker too, recognising that by neglecting her work in favour of the other better known Objectivists they were neglecting one of the great American modernists. This new *Collected Works* provides us with a great opportunity: to try to trace in her penetrating lyrics the peculiar method of their almost constant success. This will entail, again and probably not for the last time, a confrontation with what alienated her, from publication, from later critical attention, and from the corruptions of post-War American culture.

Late Blessings

IAN TROMP

W. S. Merwin, *The Pupil*
Alfred A. Knopf, $23.00, ISBN 037541276X
***W. S. Merwin: A Listener's Guide* (compact disc and 25pp leaflet)**
Copper Canyon Press, $12.00, ISBN 155659996X

"FOR THE ANNIVERSARY OF MY DEATH", a poem from W. S. Merwin's 1967 volume *The Lice*, concluded speaking of "bowing not knowing to what". Nearly forty years on, the poet returns to this idea in a poem entitled "Just Now", a title that resonantly runs together senses of "a moment ago" and a quietly emphatic directive to attend only to this moment, an attitude basic to Merwin's longstanding practice of Zen. The poem captures a moment of clarity in which "it seems to me / that there has been something simpler than I could ever believe / simpler than I could have begun to find words for"; it ends asking, "by what name can I address it now holding out my thanks". This sense of gratitude to a graceful source and support of and for our lives has recurred throughout Merwin's writing; in *The Pupil*, it takes the particular form of appreciating that he is the recipient of "late blessings":

>   … I
> have been standing here in this light
> seeing this moon and its one star
> while the cows went home with their bells
> and the sheep were folded and gone
> and the elders fell silent one
> after another and loved souls
> were no longer seen and my hair
> turned white and I was looking up
> out of a time of late blessings
>
>   ("First Sight")

In a poem from his 1999 collection *The River Sound*, Merwin used a description of generations of animals and people walking a lane to evoke a sense of the marking of time in landscape – a scale more patient and enduring than our familiar human one:

> the walls of the lane
> are older than anyone can understand
> and the lane must have been a path a long time
> before the first stones were raised beside it
> and must have been a trail from the river
> up through the trees for an age before that
> one hoof one paw one foot before another
> the way they went is all that is still there

In *The Pupil*, Merwin's timescales are vastly expanded. He still evokes geologic time passing – as in "Worn", which describes a worn stone doorsill by recalling "the stones lifted out / of the ground and set into walls / for a while waiting to return" – but he also, now, encompasses far greater chronological sweeps. It seems the poet spends a lot of time looking up, observing cosmic light, which indirectly evokes time and distance: the stars which we see burned in another time, and their light has crossed vast distances and thousands of years to reach us in ours. *The Pupil's* final poem, "This January", blends the universal and personal scales of time; describing winter stars, Merwin writes that they

> . . . are still forming
> the heavy elements
> that when the stars are gone
> fly up as dust finer
> by many times than a hair
> and recognize each other
> in the dark traveling
> at great speed and becoming
> our bodies in our time
> looking up after rain
> in the cold night together

The elements that constitute our bodies originated "in the dark", and we are not different from the substance of the stars or the material of the world we inhabit. This realisation is an aspect of the disposition of "holding out . . . thanks" and "bowing not knowing to what".

Copper Canyon's *Listener's Guide* includes Merwin reading "For the Anniversary of My Death", along with forty-three other poems from the course of his long career. The variousness of style among the poems gives a good overview of Merwin's output, and it is delightful to hear the poet reading his own work – for one thing, since he has so long eschewed traditional punctuation and lineation for a distinctive syllabic line, it is useful to hear his own pacing and pausing in reading poems long-familiar on the page. The leaflet accompanying the CD includes a short, thoughtful essay by Sam Hamill (founder and publisher of Copper Canyon Press), an undated few remarks from Merwin under the title "On the Making of Poems", and two important statements that he made in the 1970s, in response to being awarded the Pulitzer Prize, and in advance of giving a public reading at the State University of New York. These two texts are an interesting choice for a recording released so many years later, and their inclusion underlines a social engagement that has long characterised Merwin's writing, but is usually less directly expressed in his poems.

In "On the Making of Poems", Merwin writes that "A poem begins to be a poem when a sequence of words starts giving off what you might describe as a kind of electric charge, when it begins to have a life of its own that I sense the way I would if I suddenly picked up a shorted electric wire". The charge imparted by the poems of *The Pupil* issues from the near-perfect balance and ease of their language – it is a charge of wonderment and fit, rather than of sheer energy. They are not just a vehicle for their imagery of light; they are themselves alight with the quiet candescence of a master poet.

Water's Soliloquy

DERYN REES-JONES
Alice Oswald, *Dart*
Faber, £8.99, ISBN 057121410X

A CURIOUS AND brilliant hybrid, in which ghosts of *The Waste Land* meet *Under Milk Wood,* with a dash of *The Waves,* and something not a million miles away from mass observation exercises in the 1930s (the poet was two years recording the stories of people who are credited at the front of the volume), and occasional moments of Ted Hughes (I'm thinking particularly of *Wodwo*), Alice Oswald has sought in her book-length poem *Dart* to chart what she calls in her preface the "mutterings of a river" in an attempt to draw "a songline from source to sea".

Like the Derwent, the river with which Wordsworth begins his earliest version of *The Prelude*, the Dart's name – as one of Oswald's quirky, inset glosses informs us – derives from an ancient word for an oak tree. Where Wordsworth used the Derwent as a reflection of his burgeoning mind, Oswald seems to be offering the lives of those who live and work alongside the River Dart as a collective version of a historical moment in which biography, and autobiography, which become our histories, are scrutinised in relation to nature and thus redefine it. The natural world is not offered as an easy answer to our understanding, Oswald seems to be suggesting, but it is, in our *imagining* of it, a contributing factor in our ability to place ourselves in the world:

> And then I saw the river's dream-self walk
> Down to the ring mesh netting by the bridge
> To feel the edge of shingle brush the edge
> Of sleep and float a world up like a cork
> Out of its body's liquid dark.
> Like in a waterfall one small twig caught
> Catches a stick , a straw, a sack , a mesh
> Of leaves, a fragile wickerwork of floodbrash,
> I saw all things catch and reticulate
> Into this dreaming of the Dart
> That sinks like a feather falls, not quite

In full possession of its weight.

Thus *Dart* might be seen to offer us what Jonathan Bate in his *Song of the Earth* refers to as "history through topography". And if the river offers us a slice of time, a vision of England – as the oak tree reference might suggest – it is one which shows both harmony and disunity. Oblique references to war riddle the poem, focusing specifically on the turbulence at the point at which the East Dart meets the West Dart – something we can hardly fail to read at some level both as a commentary on wider global concerns, as well as an advocation of the intermingling and assimilation of disparate registers and voices, science and mythology through which our histories are recorded.

Despite or perhaps because of this, Oswald's role as overseer of the poem seems to be an attempt to find a voice – for herself, and for nature – a voice which constantly becomes redefined in its very interaction with the human and the historical. "This is me" she writes at the end of the poem:

> anonymous, water's soliloquy,
>
> All names, all voices, Slip-Shape, this is Proteus,
> Whoever that is, the shepherd of the seals,
> Driving my many selves from cave to cave.

It's no accident that mutter and mute are not far away from each other etymologically, and through the muttering river Oswald implicitly also asks us to rethink important questions about the relationship of the feminine to both language and nature in the twenty-first century. *Dart* is many things: ambitious, lyrical, clever, suggestive, complex, sometimes exquisitely beautiful. It is hard to think of many contemporary poems which have such range, and carry such authority and vision.

A Treatment for Anxiety

CAITRIONA O'REILLY

Simon Armitage, *The Universal Home Doctor*
Faber, £12.99, ISBN 0571215335

"IT WAS THE RAINFOREST, so guess what, it pissed down", writes Simon Armitage in "The Wood for the Trees". There is something familiar about this tone: masculine, "well hard", similar to a number of his poetic contemporaries. Finding such a writer in a rain forest raises expectations of something viciously anti-pastoral – but Armitage disarms by unpredictability. What continues to mark him out from his contemporaries is the rigour and strangeness of his writing, and the pervasive sense of anxiety, even dread, underlying his poetry. His colloquialism and his attraction to cliché (*à la* Paul Muldoon) are thus continually set within unexpected and subversive contexts, as when "The Wood for the Trees" metamorphoses into a mantra-like meditation on trust, before culminating in a "High Windows" vision:

> Then I wondered
> about home, the long journey backwards, and wandered
>
> down to the stream for a drink. What followed the taste
> was a sense of calm – calmness in its raw state
>
> and a quietness almost internally near.
> Then distant thoughts were suddenly blindingly clear.

In terms of style, Armitage bears superficial comparison with the more facile, less successful, and late Larkin of "High Windows" or "Love Again", the Larkin who had already fatally lost his nerve. But the comparison is a truly superficial one, since Armitage is undoubtedly the braver writer. Poems like "Birthday", "The Nerve Conduction Studies", "The Jay" or "Chainsaw versus the Pampas Grass" register the intense unease of the vulnerable body and the fallible mind, in language which is unflinching, defiant, and conscious of its own proximity to failure, but determined nevertheless to run risks. The last poem in *The Universal Home Doctor*, "Incredible", is an explicit statement on the subject, with the poet considering the inevitable "obsolescence of flesh and bone" amidst disturbing *Alice in Wonderland* shifts in scale and perspective. Even inside this dehumanising relativity he is determined to persist:

> Lifetimes went past. With the critical mass
> of hardly more than the thought of a thought
> I kept on, headlong, to vanishing point.
> I looked for an end, for some dimension
> to hold hard and resist. But I still exist.

What is refreshing about Armitage is that in the face of such exemplary postmodern anxieties, he has become neither a facile moralist nor a preening stylist. Instead, his poems go on exploring their imaginative territory with pioneering relish. He keeps company with "the deep-sea diver or astronaut" as well as with the decidedly anti-heroic protagonists of "The Laughing Stock", a funny, angry vision of a debased British underclass who "lounge / on broken settees, scoff bite-size portions of chocolate and fat, / crack open a tinnie or two. Skin up. Channel hop." Armitage's examinations of the meaning of Englishness highlight his ambitions as a writer, but can also risk sounding opportunistic. "The English" reads like pastiche Larkin, and "It Could Be You" like Glyn Maxwell, but Armitage is at his sharpest in "The Twang", where he re-imagines St. Patrick's Day in New York as a celebration of English culture: "They'd dyed the Hudson with cochineal and chalk. / Bulldogs were arse-to-mouth in Central Park". As well as taking a deft side-swipe at one of the more nauseating manifestations of international oirishry, this poem expresses the peculiar queasiness of English nationalism, that love that dare not speak its name, in its final stanza:

> A paper dragon tripped down Lexington, its tongue
> truly forked. Two hands thrust from its open throat:
> in the left, a red nose; in the right, a collection box
> for the National Trust. I mean the National Front.

What remains intriguing about this poem is Armitage's avoidance of the obvious reversal of "National Trust" and "National Front" in the last line; as it is the line reads less like a self-correction, more like an intensification. Armitage also satirises the Brit Art phenomenon in his prose poem "Assault on the Senses", a parody of an exhibition catalogue, in which a description of each exhibit is followed by the inevitable words "private collection". One of the exhibits, entitled "Shit for Brains", consists of : "mixed media: glass case containing baked life-size brain sculpted in artist's own excrement, positioned on domestic 'Libra' weighing scales, overbalanced by tin of dog meat. Private collection." Belly-laughs aside, Armitage has made his point well.

Easily the best poem in the volume, however is "The Back Man", a bizarre excursus on one of Armitage's principal themes; the ludicrous disparity between imaginative wildness and social compromise. The poem opens with its speaker walking, "the last in line" through an exotic reserve when he feels himself attacked from behind by a nightmarish apparition: "and I saw in my mind's eye the carved mask / of its face, the famous robe of black fur, / the pins and amulets of its claws and feet . . .". Surprisingly, he is physically unharmed, and the poem then shifts to a litany in which he details the precise nature of his victimisation:

> not escaping into freedom or peacetime
> but trousering readies extruded from cashpoints,
> eating the thick air that blasts the escarpment,
> not rising to the bait of a fur coat
> but yacking on the cordless, cruising Ceefax,
> checking the pollen-count and the long range forecast [...]

The poem conveys the suffocation, panic, and frustration of its subject by a minute and carefully controlled accumulation of detail. "The Back Man", like the book as a whole, provides a powerful revision of Larkin's poised compositions and their speakers' patiently diminished expectations.

The Smeared Vision

STEPHEN JAMES

Geoffrey Hill, *The Orchards of Syon*
Penguin, £9.99, ISBN 0141009918

THE POETRY OF Geoffrey Hill is often misunderstood. In part, this is a matter of readers not recognising the extent to which Hill wishes us to experience and consciously explore mis-understanding. Too frequently, the drive to work out what Hill's poetry means masks the possibility that the unresolved response may be a salutary one, that failures to comprehend are an integral part of the reading process. These shortcomings are registered in the writing process too: Hill recognises the distinction between apprehension and comprehension and composes poetry that makes an exhibition of its struggle from the former towards the unreachable latter. His work displays knowledge – ostentatiously and often forbiddingly – but it is also preoccupied with the limitations of the knowable. This is true to a peculiar degree of his latest book-length poem, *The Orchards of Syon*, a poem that is admittedly hard to comprehend but the sense and spirit of which one may nonetheless apprehend, become sympathetically involved with and emotionally stirred by.

Hill's new work explores the nature of intuition and intimation. It meditates death and the possible hereafter. It considers, too, how illusory one's purchase may be on life, one's sense of self, one's environment, one's memories. There is sadness and beauty, remorse and consolation, in the verse. The poem both laments the limits of comprehension and promotes the condition of unknowing that is a necessary part of a self-transcending, or spiritual, experience. The reader in turn is required both to rise to the interpretive challenge posed by the poem's allusive and polyphonic manner and to contemplate the significance – even the value – of the confusion experienced in undertaking this challenge. Paradoxically, difficulty unites poet and reader, rather than driving them apart. The reader's encounter with the intractable and the ineffable is Hill's also.

Certainly, Hill's poetry is learned and demanding and recessively referential, but I do not ever get the sense (as some readers evidently do) that Hill talks down to his audience; there may at times be austerity and archness in the manner of delivery but these consciously cultivated mannerisms are bound up with a tendency to self-deflation and are complicated by comic registers. Nor is Hill's work condescending; rather, it is braced against the conde-scension implicit in linguistic looseness, reductive jargon, and the "tyranny" of mass media simplifications. Hill laments historical ignorance and cultural complacency and forces us to consider how the index of these demeaning traits is to be found in linguistic imprecision. We cannot be inattentive to the connotations of any single word when reading a Geoffrey Hill poem. His exactitude regarding language makes the reading process an exacting one, yet what this conveys is not disdain but, rather, respect. To make demands on the intelligence is to respect that intelligence.

Hill's often-quoted contention that "genuinely difficult art is truly democratic" is more beguiling. In the case of his own "genuinely difficult" work, the "democratic" impulse might be located in etymological sensitivity, since language, for Hill, is a common entitlement, and coming to understand the history and workings of that language a form of self-enfranchisement. To have a simplified, reductive sense of language, by contrast, is to be controlled and constricted by the very words one employs – to be disempowered. Hill's long-standing preoccupation with an ideal sense of the "common weal" ("weal" meaning "well-being") – a preoccupation that came to the fore in *Canaan* in 1996 and that has remained prominent in his work since then – is bound up with a resistance to linguistic ignorance. To Hill's mind, this ignorance bespeaks a cultural deprivation, a condition which allows for "the people" to be misled and exploited. The tyrannical forces that carry out such exploitation are the forces of the corporate media, of patronising populism, of unexamined platitudes. Hill's new work steadfastly resists such forces – although, it is worth noting, with less vituperation and outrage than is to be found in the preceding book-length poems, *The Triumph of Love* (1998) and *Speech! Speech!* (2000).

This concern for language as a concern for commonality is implicit – obliquely – in the very title of Hill's new work: *The Orchards of Syon*. The *OED* informs us that Syon is an archaic word for Zion, the name of one of the hills of Jerusalem, on which the city of David was built, and which became the centre of Jewish life and worship. Yet to enquire further into the word is to discover that, in biblical and derived usage, Syon stands allusively for the house or household of God and hence connotes, variously: the Israelites and their religious system; the Christian Church; heaven as the final home of believers; a place of worship or meeting-house; or a form of social organisation conceived of as an ultimate goal. To know this is to recognize that the term Zionism – which the callousness of linguistic ignorance often reduces to notions of the factional, the militant and the nationalistic – conceals the inclusive, communal and even (potentially) inter-denominational ideal to be found at the root of the word. The archaism of Hill's chosen spelling is not wilful; properly considered, it does not obscure but clarify. Responding to the very title of Hill's work may involve an encounter with difficulty, but the demands Hill places on the reader should not be misprised as a form of authorial tyranny. The impulse behind the difficulty is democratic – albeit in a peculiar way.

Hill's poem is drawn towards Syon, a locus of individual salvation and a putative place of common belonging. It does not, however, attempt to imagine the notional "house" itself. (Might such an attempt be for Hill some form of blasphemy? Like purporting to describe the face of God? Or peering inside the tabernacle?) Rather, it strives to depict the orchards surrounding the house. Yet these orchards – being notional – cannot be seen, merely apprehended, and the only means of apprehension available are derived from images of earthly landscapes. And so Hill's struggle to perceive an unambiguously beneficent, bountiful realm – some kind of second Eden – is constantly interfered with by glimpses of the fallen world. This new work is not, as one piece of publicity has claimed, Hill's *Paradiso*. It would be more accurate to say that the work is tormented by the near-impossibility of apprehending the paradisal state. Hill's poem explores scarred and spoiled terrains: "skeletal" orchards, "wintry swamp thickets", icy landscapes, locations "glutted with spillage" where "puffballs" are "reared on dust". It glimpses "The Wood of the Suicides" with its "leaves / hanging blood-brown" (an allusion to Canto XIII of the *Inferno*) and casts an affrighted eye over many other sites of devastation past and present – including, briefly, the troubled "Holy Land" where the promise of neither Syon nor Zion offers a credible and practical solution to an intractable political crisis. The creation of the state of Israel is seen as a "pledged curse" bestowed by the international community, the inverse of an inclusive and harmonious society.

Yet balanced against such gloomy vistas are evocations of moments when the world brightens and a transient apprehension of nature's magnificence becomes available:

> How beautiful the world unrecognized

through most of seventy years, the may-tree filling
with visionary silent laughter.

Even here, though, the recompense is elusive: Hill's words might prompt one to visualize blossom frothing and swaying on a tree in spring time, as if at once the source and the embodiment of the beholder's happiness, yet the connection between such an image and an experience of "silent laughter" is ultimately ineffable. This is the point of the "visionary": it cannot be articulated or transcribed. And so Hill makes poetry out of the impossibility of rendering in language that which he perceives. Every moment of vision is a moment not easily visualized, the product of shadow-play and half-light, the stuff of paradox: "the light / enters upon its own darkness and falls / mute"; "I shall promote our going and coming, / as shadows, in expressive light"; plants are "light-endowed / among the natural shades and shadows"; "accustomed ratios of shine to shadow" are "reversed". Paradox also governs Hill's idea of "The Orchards of Syon" themselves. He describes them at one point as "tenebrous thresholds / of illumination", as if to suggest that the brightness which one hopes to access can only be approached and cannot (at least in this life) be attained. This brightness might be the light of the next world, the "fixed home" towards which so many lines of Hill's mortality-minded poem incline, or it might be the light of a social ideal as intimated by works of "extraordinary / common goodness" in the present life; either way, the point of entry is "tenebrous" and can be reached only by traversing all those unlit regions which the many sites of desolation and despoliation in the poem represent.

Hill sees the world through a glass darkly. Each vision is a "smeared vision", the product of blurred perception. And yet Hill insists that "blurring sharpens" and writes of a particular "revelation" being "blurred afresh by rain" – as if blurring is an act of freshening, the clarifying vision a matter of losing focus. This is of a part with the willed letting-go of the comprehending faculty which the poem advocates, with the faith-over-reason philosophy of the medieval theologian Thomas Bradwardine whom Hill summons in one of the epigraphs to this book (and in other works), and with the emphasis Hill places on pre-rational childhood wonder. One of the recurrent analogies for the unreachable Orchards is "Goldengrove", that elusive realm sought after in Gerard Manley Hopkins's poem "Spring and Fall: To a Young Child". The poem describes the grieving of a young girl, Margaret, for the autumnal destruction of a woodland scene but it does so from an adult perspective, one that knows the spectacle of falling leaves serves as an analogy for mankind's fallen condition and for encroaching death. The poem laments the loss of the pre-lapsarian innocence supposedly represented by a child in the springtime of her life and yet Hopkins remains profoundly ambivalent about the respective virtues of innocence and knowledge:

Ah! ás the heart grows older
It will come to such sights colder
By and by, nor spare a sigh
Though worlds of wanwood leafmeal lie;
And yet, you will weep and know why.

In line with Hill's notion of "smeared vision", here weeping blurs the perspective in such a way as to sharpen it. And yet, the wisdom gained comes at a cost: the heart is "colder" and the response to the messages of the natural world less intuitive. Hill shares Hopkins's double-edged stance, seeking both to know and to surrender the knowing faculty. That the reader too is meant to share this paradoxical condition can be inferred from Hill's self-conscious construction of a pairing of locations: "Goldengrove" and "Silvertown". If the former place represents a notional realm to which one might respond imaginatively and instinctively, then the latter is its factual counterpart. Silvertown is a place in Essex that was largely destroyed on 19 January, 1917, when a large stock of explosives ignited in a munitions factory. The contrast between this incontrovertibly real and locatable incident and the allegorical world of Goldengrove could hardly be starker.

Responding to Hill's poem, then, involves negotiating between the pursuit of necessary knowledge – as of historical events too easily forgotten – and the virtue of relinquishing rational control. Moments of apprehension are held in the balance with acts of attestation. Not that it is always easy to discern the real from the imagined in a poem so haunted by phantoms and mirages, illusions and vanishing tricks, fantasies and dreams. One of the many literary texts it invokes is *La vida es sueño* (*Life is a Dream*), a baroque philosophical romance by the great seventeenth-century Spanish playwright Calderón de la Barca. The ideas explored in this play define both the quest of Hill's poem and, one presumes, the progression towards understanding it would ideally provoke in the reader. The play charts the difficult spiritual journey of its protagonist, Segismundo, towards enlightenment and redemption. It teaches us that life is the product of flux and mutability, and that the material, sensory world is comprised merely of lures and deceptions, yet it stresses that this is all we have. Calderón's message is a riddling one: we need to become aware both that we are dreaming and that we cannot wake up from the dream. Just so, *The Orchards of Syon* registers, and demands from its readers, the restless operations of the intellect while not purporting to claim – nor expecting its readers to presume – full rational comprehension of what is encountered. Hill's new work constitutes a bewildering but beautiful and moving verse-dream. Every true critical response needs to begin by registering what it feels like to be inside the dream, and by apprehending why one is there.

Seduction and Betrayal

MUTLU KONUK BLASING

Nazim Hikmet, *Beyond the Walls: Selected Poems*
Translated by Ruth Christie, Richard McKane, and Talat Sait Halman.
Anvil, £11.95, ISBN 0856 463 299

"GREAT POET" AND "GREATEST POET", Nazim Hikmet wrote, are "strange" and "embarrassing" terms. Yet just such words apply to him, both because of his genius and because of the way he responded to the importance of his historical moment. Hikmet belongs to the generation of poets born around the turn of the last century, poets whose lives and work are inextricable from momentous global events, and his life and work unfolded on the international stage. But his life and work are also inextricable from the founding and early history of the Turkish Republic. He came of age as a poet at the moment when Turkey was constructing itself as a modern, secular state. For him, the project of a modern Turkish poetry was politicized from the beginning; it was inseparable from the project of imagining a Turkish national and cultural identity.

As Turkey came to define itself in the 1930s, Hikmet's radical politics became dangerous, and he paid dearly for his belief that communism would achieve a just society. He served a thirteen-year sentence – during his most poetically productive period – as a political prisoner, and spent his last thirteen years in exile. He was stripped of his Turkish citizenship and is buried in Moscow, where he died at sixty-one in 1963. Partly because his persecution lends his words authority, Hikmet continues to be a dangerous and controversial figure. His work is still excluded from Turkish school books, and the posthumous restoration of his citizenship and the disposition of his remains are hotly debated issues in Turkey, on which political parties take official positions.

Hikmet articulates a moment of linguistic and literary as well as political change. He brought Turkish poetry into the twentieth century, changing the very idea of what could be said poetically in Turkish. His new forms, he said, were necessitated by his revolutionary content rather than by a desire to destroy traditional values. He made poetry in Turkish deal with subjects it had not addressed before. No doubt his first-hand acquaintance with Russian avant-garde poets and playwrights in Moscow in the early twenties inspired his formal innovations, but he himself said that his Futurist phase lasted a very short time. His page looks modern in its typographical arrangement, but it is designed to orchestrate the phrase units of spoken Turkish with the quantitative meters of Ottoman poetry and the syllabics, rhymes, and repetitions of Turkish folk poetry. These distinct traditions of written and oral poetry have different metrical systems, prosodic resources, vocabularies, and even syntax. Hikmet's page is a score for redistributing these traditions and aural memories. Such a combination was unthinkable before him and has proved impossible after him.

Hikmet's content is always at least implicitly revolutionary, and he does have some dreary propaganda poems written in his years in Russia. These are not what make him dangerous. A lot of other people have said the same things interminably. Rather it's his intimacy with the innate and innately conservative authority of the mother tongue – its "beautiful necessities" and its traditions – that makes him dangerous, because it also makes him irresistible. His most powerful poems are not at all tendentious; they are disarming expressions of the universal human desire for freedom, justice, and happiness. His language absorbs and naturalizes his ideology. This is a formidable power for a poet to hold.

I know from experience – I am myself with Randy Blasing a translator of Hikmet – that the historical texture of his language does not translate, any more than the semiotic code and code-dependent effects do. Among the distinctive features of Turkish are its agglutinative structure and its vowel harmony – features that make rhymes, even multisyllabic rhymes, seem inevitable. Thus Hikmet's deceptively simple language and accessible content make it even harder to sound the poetry of his words in English, where rhymes are hardly inevitable. Even so, Hikmet commands a voice and an authority that do come through in translation and make him worth reading in any language.

Beyond the Walls collects the work of three translators; only eleven poems out of the total of ninety-six are translated by the one native Turkish speaker among them, Talat Halman. Previous English translations of Hikmet have been done either by, or in collaboration with, native speakers. Yet Ruth Christie and Richard McKane, who learned Turkish as adults, state that they "applied a golden rule of translation, of not reading the precursor translations while we were translating". I find this baffling. I should think the responsibility of any translator – as of any scholar or poet – is "to find out what has been done, better than it can ever be done again, and to find out what remains for us to do", as Ezra Pound wrote.

Certainly, Christie and McKane's irresponsibility toward the originals is baffling. I will limit myself to a single example. A major late poem, the longest in this selection, is entitled "Saman Sarisi" – literally, "Straw-Blonde". This gets rendered as "Flaxen Hair," which calls to mind a different type of blonde altogether. Also, the original title does not mention "hair"; it could be describing a patch of colour. Hikmet's poem, running to twelve pages, is a *tour de force*. It concerns time, how it feels to be both chasing and fleeing time as it slips away from and speeds towards you, and it has a breathless, accelerating pace and a building rhythmic momentum. It has no punctuation whatsoever, but its syntax is clear, and it flows and reads fast. The translator must somehow build syntactic pauses into the rhythmic movement, and the rhythm must carry the sense. Yet this translator makes the choice to fully punctuate the poem. The choppy little sentences – the first six lines all end in periods – interrupt the poem's vitally relentless rhythm and headlong movement. I can think of no justification for such a willful betrayal of the original, and here, as elsewhere, Christie and McKane's translations would have benefited greatly from their consulting existing versions.

Things to Do in Llandudno When You're Dead

JAMES KEERY

David Constantine, *Something for the Ghosts*
Bloodaxe £7.95, ISBN 1852245905

SOMETHING HAS GONE wrong here, surely?

> The bulk, thin flora, hunched here like a crow,
> Sky red as poppy, black
> As the heart of a poppy, some long way below
> Slop, slop, the constant cuffing of the sea …
>
> Get back, on hands and knees snuffling a track
> While there's still blood in the sky, get back
> To the B&B and your scented mate
> Between silk sheets after her bath, get her on you
>
> To practise, practise, practise the kiss of life.

("On the Cliffs, Boscastle")

I don't mean the "B&B" with "silk sheets" – depends how you like your eggs, I suppose. Nor even the treatment of Hardy: the title recalls "At Castle Boterel", Hardy's name for Boscastle; the first phrase is a brusque allusion to "Beeny Cliff" ("Still in all its chasmal beauty bulks old Beeny to the sky"); and the deathless fourth line travesties "After a Journey" ("The waked birds preen and the seals flop lazily"). It's the grisly climax that upsets me. The melodramatic animality culminates in "your scented mate", but there is nothing bestial about this: "Get back … get back … get her on you"! What was he thinking of? In dire need of "the kiss of life", the speaker joins the procession of the "living dead" who people this extraordinary book.

The sea may be sloppy, but the writing isn't – every effect is calculated, including my own response. The ironies begin with the epigraph from "The Extasie": "To our bodies turn we then ..." Turn we then to the first poem, to find a "Nude", fresh from the shower, "at a meeting place / Of warm sunlight and loving admiration / And easy feeling both". Well, as Donne also said, "Full nakedness, all joys are due to thee!" Yet the peaceful, easy feeling is a set-up, a sardonic guarantee of the "prevailing mood ... of unease" announced in the blurb. The "loving admiration" becomes an obsessive voyeurism, hinted at in "Nude" – "On her back there is a man's admiration"; overt in "Sleepwalker" – "I watched her window from a vantage point"; and explicit in "Man and Wife", the narrative of a "voyeur" whose wife thinks "they should lock him up". His obsession is not with women but with "the deep unease of the marsh", where, "night after night" – perhaps under the *voyeuse* moon" of "Skylight over the Bath"? – he can persist in "Trying to see things as though he were dead and gone". Cue title poem on next page, with another walk-on role for "her feet on the cold tiles":

> Here's something for the ghosts who are
> No one now and can't come up against
> The edge of anyone else: that heavy skirt,
> Your bare cold feet come out from under it,
> Their print, black wet, on the slabs of slate ...

With hindsight, even the first line of "Nude" has a sinister ring: "How simple it is: day knocks ..." In "the arena of a performance", with "water lifted in her hands", it has to be the ghost of Lady Macbeth: "A little water clears us of this deed: / How easy is it then!" Her next words – "Hark! More knocking" – give the innocent phrase, "day knocks", a *frisson* of terror, implicating the couple in bloodshed and obsessive guilt, the keynote of the collection. (In "Jazz on the Charles Bridge", the river is "Sick of ferrying our murders to the dead sea"; in "School Parties in the Museum", "force, / Hatred, history, all that" is written-off as a record of barbarism, "black as the people's blood"; and in "Hallowe'en", the moral from the "terror" of an eclipse is bluntly drawn: "Life here's / Like that".)

By the second poem, then, Donne's "bodies" have become "ghosts" – well, okay, he did also see "the skull beneath the skin" – but wait, Constantine still hasn't finished deconstructing "Nude":

> Poor gibbering ghosts, when they have done
>
> Their best with bits of sound to shape someone
> They knew or thought they knew or wished they had
> It never amounts to anything more than this
> Ghost of a mouth with questions in such as
> Who were you and who did you think I was?

Since you ask, I thought you were one of the best poets alive, with the gift of shaping "bits of sound" into some inimitably beautiful things:

> For years now through your face the skull has shown
> Nearer than through their living surface
> The hills' bulk of dead stone ...

Finally the gap is absolute. Living
At all you were never nearly dead
And dead there is nothing
Vital of you in the abandoned face.
But the lack, the difference, has such nearness
We could almost embrace.

There, indeed, is "the skull beneath the skin", but between *A Brightness to Cast Shadows* (1980) and *Something for the Ghosts*, finally, sadly, "the gap is absolute". Consider "Dear Reader", an intriguing allegory of the birth of a new poem (reminiscent of Larkin's "Latest Face"): "Her eyes were on a page, her fingers left // The soft pulse of his silky fontanelle / To turn another page". Having weaned her first, "she began again in another situation . . . in at the seeding, // Sexing, naming, in at the jostling / Of destinies against their author". The trouble is that too many of the progeny invite the "sad diagnosis" of Plath's "Stillborn": "These poems do not live".

Not that they particularly wish to. "The Porthleven Man" is the tale of someone who swam out to sea and "never came back", except to haunt the speaker: "These nights when I wake / The Porthleven man keeps coming back to me. / I need icons, I need people to live up to / Because of your horizons, because of your western sea". So Hardy's "western sea" ("Beeny Cliff") must signify death, not love – and if that's not bad enough, this icon leaves "his zimmer . . . on the edge"! The same poem recalls Constantine's excellent second collection, *Watching for Dolphins*, with "one continuous / Making of dolphins . . . Under her pulsing moon" (it was, after all, an ageing Antony whose "delights were dolphin-like" beneath "the visiting moon"); but can we cut the zimmer out of shot?

"The Llandudno Town Band" is a *reductio ad absurdum* of Larkin's "To the Sea" in which "the same old crowd, minus the passed away" enjoy the music until "all // Not stiff for ever get to their feet". No precise casualty-figure is given, but you get the picture. Neither *Abide with Me* nor the trumpet-solo by "Our Dave" ("Art, if you like") is "much cop / Against the whole of the Irish Sea / Come very close". Again, the image of encroaching death.

"Ashes and Roses" is a gentle poem about the speaker's mother, with a moving ending: "Come home // To your empty house. He is more there than here". Sadly, though, the series of poems about a father's "ashes" – and symbolic "sacred rowan" (mountain ash) – is disfigured by morbidity. In "Ashes and Roses" it is a ghastly simile ("the bare bones of roses") that does the damage, while a poem affectionately entitled "The Crem" offers "dead bouquets on the earth like murdered birds". There is also a running contrast between images of the "fine soil" beloved of the father – "unctuous earth", "mole-tilth", etc. – and "the thin / Ash whose every mote was body once".

The rancour in these poems towards the "present occupiers" of a childhood home is generalised, in "Dominion", into a misanthropic caricature of "Man":

The truth is we're not good enough, never were,
Never will be, we're not fit, we don't fit in,
 Nothing will live with us except the viruses
And dogs and lice, nothing likes us down here,
Everything else is subtler, finer, fitter than us.

Come off it, "Our Dave"!

Le Livre est sur la Table

JOHN PILLING

Twentieth-Century French Poems, edited by Stephen Romer
Faber, £10.99, ISBN 0571196837

ANTHOLOGIES LIVE OR die at the mercy of a quixotic pleasure principle. Necessarily, anthologists have to indulge their enthusiasms while at the same time meeting the requirements of coverage and comprehensiveness. There are – though there are not very many – classics in the genre, some as long ago, it almost seems, as Confucius's: *The Golden Treasury, Other Men's Flowers*. More than a few of these are *FBOs* – *Faber Book of . . .* ; *Modern Verse* and *Twentieth-Century Verse* are the two which many of us grew up with. For the Europeans one tended to turn to other imprints. But here is an exception that has been widely, and for the most part warmly, welcomed. "Every contributor to it deserves our thanks", wrote Anthony Sheridan in a letter to the *TLS*; "the best kind of manifesto because it makes points without having to score them" (the ubiquitous Adam Phillips, in the *Guardian*) and "a useful book" (Alistair Elliot, in the *TLS,* lamenting that it might have been "more useful" still) confirm the general tendency. This is not, though – or at least not explicitly – an *FBO*. We are not being invited, not being encouraged either, to compare it with an obvious competitor in the field, Paul Auster's bilingual *Random House Book of Twentieth Century French Poetry* of twenty years ago. Faber have simply given Steven Romer – to his pleasure and surprise no doubt – a blank cheque to fill in with anything and everything of quality translated from the immensely rich vein of French twentieth-century poetry, with double the space of comparable (but en face) enterprises; although, as Elliot quite rightly remarks, "few will want to have the English only".

Auster, with 300 pages at his disposal (600/2), chooses 48 poets; Romer, with less than 200, 54, with an earlier starting-pont (Valéry, rather than Apollinaire) and, naturally enough, a more recent endpoint. These bald figures and the distribution indicate that Romer, poet for poet, must be skimpier than Auster; and so it proves. The numbers game also discloses that Romer has dropped (or for some reason excluded) 17 of Auster's complement, most of them post-war poets, a group naturally more likely to fluctuate as taste changes. He therefore ends up with no less than 23, almost half his total, who are not to be found in Auster. Reason enough to own both. "Extraordinary", wrote Beckett's Molloy, "how mathematics help you to know yourself", or at least to get a grip upon what's where. Beckett, as it happens, is in Romer, with the "Afar A Bird" *foirade* which – like the extracts from Artaud's *The Mountain of Signs* and Raymond Roussel's *Locus Solus* – looks questionable in principle, though in practice it works well with Beckett, since the *foirade* is only one of a kind, whereas the others are parts of evolving wholes.

Who's in, who's out? Notable absentees are O. V. de L. Milosz, an acquired taste certainly, and something of a special case, and two Andrés, Frénaud and Du Bouchet, in spite of excellent versions by Keith Bosley and by Auster that would no doubt have been made available. Léon-Paul Fargue is another casualty. Of Romer's inclusions particularly welcome are Lorand Gaspar, Léopold Senghor and Jean Tardieu, and eight of his poets are women, four of them from a single source (Martin Sorell's *Elles* published by Exeter University Press). Included amongst them, though from the more remote source of Box Editions of Brockport, is the excellent Canadian poet Anne Hébert.

Which are the success stories? Cendrars certainly (by various hands); less predictably,

Max Jacob (ditto). Alan Jenkins's versions of Larbaud are exceptionally good, and Nathaniel Tarn's Segalens still look strong more than thirty years on. In the cases of Segalen and, to a lesser extent, Jacob, a rising in the poet's own stock may make a difference. Poets of the very highest quality naturally suffer proportionately more losses in the conversion process. Reverdy, alas, has still to find his ideal other (though the Martin Bell translations from the Whiteknights Press deserve to be better known). Only one of Romer's Valéry selections is at all familiar, as was obviously a deliberate choice ("I wanted to reveal the Valéry of the *Cahiers*, or *Notebooks*"); this said, Elliot quite justifiably considers the six prose poems chosen from them "indifferent", and it must also be said that the endlessly fascinating *Cahiers* are, unfortunately, endless once embarked upon. Romer's selection from Apollinaire (even with "The Pretty Redhead") is also rather eccentric. Since Saint-John Perse remains (in English at least) a victim of his own rhetoric, perhaps only Yves Bonnefoy, very aptly in view of his stature as a translator from English, breaks this law of diminishing returns.

Which translators make a special impact, other than those already singled out? Romer himself certainly (Robert Desnos; Jacques Dupin); Paul Auster (Dupin again); David Gascoyne (Supervielle, Éluard, Jouve); Lawrence Ferlinghetti (Prévert); Derek Mahon (Jaccottet); Samuel Beckett (one, but only one, of the Éluard versions first published in the special Surrealist number of Edward Titus's *This Quarter* in September 1932, where they were singled out as "superlative"). Nothing exactly unknown here, though each interested party will inevitably know some better than others. Romer must have rubbed his hands with glee at the riches available to him in undertaking this commission. Even so, *Twentieth-Century French Poems* is undoubtably a job well done.

A Walk Through the Woods

JOHN REDMOND

W. S. Merwin, *The Mays of Ventadorn*
National Geographic Directions, U.S. $20.00, ISBN 0792265386
Vona Groarke, *Flight*
Gallery, £7.95, ISBN 1852353082
Eiléan Ní Chuilleanáin, *The Girl Who Married the Reindeer*
Gallery, £7.95, ISBN 1852353031
John Montague, *Selected Poems*
Penguin, £8.99, ISBN 014029712X
Mark Doty, *Source*
Cape, £8.00, ISBN 022406228X
Peter Robinson, *About Time Too*
Carcanet, £8.95, ISBN 1857545109
Peter Levi, *Viriditas*
Anvil, £7.95, ISBN 0856463310
Iain Crichton Smith, *A Country for Old Men and My Canadian Uncle*
Carcanet, £7.95, ISBN 1857544749

SEAMUS HEANEY'S ACCOUNTS of his childhood experience are often so eerily universal that they feel like ancient parables – particularly striking is his description of getting lost in a field of tall crops. Fascinated by the green sunlit web which closed over him, he lingered inside it, contentedly alone. Later when he heard adults searching for him, their voices getting closer and closer, he began to cry. It's a version of pastoral oddly mirrored in *The Mays of Ventadorn* when W. S. Merwin, thinking of his childhood in Pennsylvania, remembers an unusual clearing in the woods:

> Light came through the green of all the leaves and the grass. The sounds were furred, as though they were coming across water, or echoed around a corner, or remembered … I did not want my name to come to me there from anywhere else, and I did not want to call out to somewhere else from there.

In each case the adult writer registers nostalgia for the child's powerful fantasy of becoming a self-sufficient world. Some feelings and states – innocence, purity, fertility for instance – are so long associated with pastoral that we encounter them with a sense of rediscovery, of having known them always; this brief ecstatic loneliness is another. Merwin is seeking to explain his feelings for southwest France – and by extension for the poetry of the troubadours – to show how his falling in love both with the landscape and its most characteristic poetry was mixed with a primal feeling of recognition.

Written in calmly enthusiastic prose, *The Mays of Ventadorn* is a mixture of biographical essay, literary history and travel book. It is part of a series, published by National Geographic Directions, where well-known writers (including David Mamet, Paul Theroux and Peter Carey) are asked to meditate on their favourite landscapes. Merwin, a senior American poet, lived in southwest France for eleven years and his affectionate rendering of this overlooked rural area – at once tumbledown and mysterious, its heritage threatened by modern agricultural methods – bears comparison with Hughes's portrait of north Devon in *Moortown Diary*. A fine book, it also focuses on his favourite troubadour poet, Bernart de Ventadorn and includes some of his poems – still remarkably fresh – from the twelfth century.

In Heaney's poetry the use of pastoral has evolved from an early defensive innocence to something more open, abstract and knowing. The verbal habits which reflect this maturing can be found, at secondhand, in the younger generation of Irish poets. Vona Groarke's third collection, *Flight*, is an example. Heaney's Larkinesque use of negative adjectives is especially noticeable – a partial list includes "uncut", "unlit", "unruffled", "unstooped", "untallied", "uninscribed", "unearmarked", "unsworn", and "unfathomable". Taken together with her repeated use of "nothing" ("It was something of nothing", "the measure of nothing", "In those days nothing came of anything"), and her playing on unheard melodies ("a promise almost made", "what was never said", "what's possible / elsewhere"), *Flight* builds its nest in negative space.

Looking at current poetry from Ireland, one notices younger poets from the Republic are developing new styles by mixing the influence of their Northern elders in different quantities. Groarke may not mean the opening line of "Thistle" ("It's hard to get away from hay these days") as a playful nod to Muldoon's influence, but he is certainly present in individual poems like "Currency" and "White Noise", and more generally in the widespread use of renewed colloquialism ("Something begun and veering off at once // as though to double back would be the point of it"). "Or to Come", the poem in *Flight* most strenuously volunteering for the anthologies, recalls not only Mahon's handling of Yeatsian big stanzas in "A Disused Shed in Co. Wexford", it borrows that poem's tone and subject-matter: "There are always unvisited corners / where the only sound is the turn taken by dandelions / or a robin rustling in the aftergrass nearby".

Groarke is a talented poet with a fine ear, yet her individuality is lost in the book's dutifully accumulated mannerisms. This is particularly obvious when she is read alongside a more established writer like Eiléan Ní Chuilleanáin. While both negotiate smalltown Ireland through a lyric I-persona, Ní Chuilleanáin has the persuasive vision which Groarke lacks. *The Girl Who Married the Reindeer* is an oblique, almost obscure, collection. We come to know Ní Chuilleanáin's highly ritualized world rather better than we remember individual poems. Peirce says somewhere that a measure of belief is when it becomes a habit; Ní Chuilleanáin believes, above all, in belief, exploring it through ancient habits of folklore and religion: compass-points, fair-greens, crossroads, "the only boy with six sisters". As in Synge, all the props (table, cup, rope) seem somehow heavier, weighted with folkloric significance. Her personae are mostly wry and distant ("I am searching for a shape, a den …") and, in a sophisticated take on Heaney's early pastoral introversion, project themselves into the natural shapes which the different poems take as structural principles – a crevasse, a cobweb, an alcove. If we can't be sure where the poems are going, we know at least that they will get there:

> … you must lie
> In the dry air of your hotel where the traffic grinds before dawn,
> The cello changing gear at the foot of the long hill,
> And think of the story of the suitors on horseback
> Getting ready to trample up the mountain of glass.

I do not know who the mounted suitors are, nor what awaits them on the mountain, but what matters – surely – is that they "trample".

One consequence of a successful poetic generation is how dated their predecessors suddenly seem. The poems of John Montague, ten years Heaney's senior, now look very dated indeed. While the coordinates of his poetry – provincial upbringing, sectarianism, travel, international sympathies and friendships – are overfamiliar (which is not his fault) the poems, purely as verbal performances, seem mediocre (which is):

> Sing an end to sectarianism,
> Fenian and Free Presbyterian,
> The punishment slowly grown
> More monstrous than the crime,
> An enormous seeping bloodstain.

This has a leaden obviousness, a quality found in the entire range of his *Selected Poems* from the overecstatic love poems ("Nightly your golden body turns / and turns in my shuddering dream") to the frantically signposted satire ("'God is Love', chalked on a grimy wall / Mocks a culture where constraint is all").

Mark Doty's *Source* displays a similar obviousness, where almost no detail is allowed to speak for itself. He is known as a poet of glitter and shine, and this book obliges with numerous production-line epiphanies. Here is his description of a group of goldfish:

> a million of them,
> a billion incipient citizens
> of a goldfish Beijing
>
> a São Paulo
> a Mexico City

A few of his poems, like the above excerpt, become strangely offensive the more one thinks about them. At a reading he once remarked, "you can never have too many sequins", a premise which this book tests to the death. *Source* looks under-revised – it's a book which might have lived with a thousand cuts:

> our spire disguised, for the season,
>
> as a minaret, or a lighthouse in Alexandria
> or the high tower room of some exiled sultan's
>
> fabled realm …

Peter Robinson's *About Time Too* offers us modest poems of domestic turmoil. He has an oppressive sense of what-might-have-been, compounded by the nervous tension of the Englishman abroad. His voice is agreeable, but the poems are often spoiled by his overlong sentences, as the conclusion of "Difficult Mornings" suggests:

> … I struggle to revise,
> revise a voice into other people's prose
> as if it were coaxing a weary lover
> till the tongue as she's spoken puts on a brave face

or exasperated, patience gone,
English itself were to sit up and tell us:
'Use me, yes, but use me well.'

The different senses of "use" give the final line resonance, but the build-up gets spoiled by syntactic and metaphoric confusion (a tongue putting on a brave face? and if "the tongue" is gendered shouldn't it be "English herself"?)

Sadly, Peter Levi and Iain Crichton Smith are no longer with us. They leave behind contrasting final books. Exploring a Georgian version of the pastoral, Levi includes phrases like "a wildness of delight" and "The spirit of Earth leaps out to fly". Containing an acrostic for Charles Causley, some untranslated French, and the rhyme of "umber" with "amber", *Viriditas* is for those who prefer the softer, mistier reaches of the pastoral:

Now trailing her dark hours the night falls
the slight leaf shivers and the last bird calls
until the sky hangs down his blackened walls
as the most ancient kings their funerals.

Iain Crichton Smith's last is a book and a half (in more than one sense): his final manuscript of short poems *A Country for Old Men* and a "much earlier" longish poem "My Canadian Uncle" (about the experiences of a Scottish immigrant to Canada). Brisk and spare, Smith writes about age with the kind of honest determination-not-to-be-fooled that reminds me of Lawrence. He can be impatiently robust ("It is time to stop writing about the Highland Clearances") but, as even the little haiku "Grass" suggests, he writes with a dignity which cannot be learned, only lived:

The grass streams all one way
but there is no dénouement
to which it points.

The Questionnaire

Poetry Review invited a number of poets to reply to the question, "Which poet, or poets, provide the measure against which you judge your writing?" Here we print a selection of responses.

MEDBH MCGUCKIAN

Georgia O'Keeffe writes: "I am trying with all my skill to do painting that is all of a woman[but]I have had to go to men as sources in my painting because the past has left so small an inheritance of women's painting that has widened life".

My life was widened recently, for a brief moment, exquisitely, poignantly, almost sexually, by standing for the first time in Coole Park, Ballylee, off the road between Galway and Limerick, under Yeats's famous and notorious tree. Which I had always avoided as a tourist attraction for visiting academics, too lofty for me. In its embrace, in his.

I say embrace because of the sense of arms and weight and sheer bodily pressure giving and not taking. Adding the delicacy of weave of summerJune light early evening through leaves, brownness, brown penniness, waterfall of bright preRaphaelite angelhair, crinoline of metallic wombspread. The copper as in coin in Heaney's Euro poem but richer red, the beech as in excoriated and only fingertippable and railed around pompously piously prudently against Paudeen me as Michael Collins's execution site far below on a sharper road bend. Maybe cordoned off at the same religious time, but not the short time I stood, not telling swanbeats, not lingering aristocratically, before tea, unable to linger, longing desperately to stay there longer, in that cave measureless, welcomed, accepted, kept out, part of and parted from it, my writing hand tracing the Cupid of his initial, thus.

Now I read of that hand, uninvited, widening, unwashed perhaps, forcing its way within the newly delivered Mary Wollstonecraft with all the arrogance of a mammogram, scattering her into a thousand costly burnished leaves. The weight of the Thames at Putney entering her like some immensely anciently beautiful tree. Brief brief kisses, the warmth of some money, letter upon letters upon letters, unopened, yearly leafing. How when she told them it was heaven, he just said, you just felt less pain, with the wine. And how today I have just scanned Thomas Ashe, in his tin cup, shirtsleeves and wide wide shoulderbraces, all the way to North Carolina: Mary's love-nest in France being let out subsequently to Thomas Russell.

DON PATERSON

Another year goes by, and another couple of poets join the ranks of those I seem no longer capable of enjoying, poets who no longer touch me. Your taste probably doesn't improve, but your attunement to mere gesture and effect probably does, or you believe it does. Funnily enough, this leaves the 40-or-so in the A-team looking all the more invulnerable; though my admiration for the work of Frost and Rilke and Dickinson and Donne has deepened over the years to the point where it no longer represents any useful mark, as I once naively thought it did.

Those poets that have fallen off the shelf . . . I certainly don't feel I've surpassed them as a poet, only outgrown as a reader. And "provide the measure" is wrong anyway. After a while it ceases to be about that sort of comparative judgement. It isn't a competition; at least not anymore. It's now a matter of negotiating some kind of authenticity for oneself in the world – and trying not to add yet another worthless artefact to it; the two projects are probably identical. You have your sociable ghosts, though. I know the criticism of Randall Jarrell well enough to know roughly what he would have said had he the misfortune to stumble on a bad poem, or possibly any poem, of mine; that's enough to ward or warn some of them off. Antonio Machado is someone else I speak to. And I'm blessed with a few friends who are honest and brilliant readers, and whose conjured presence will shout down a lot of lines before they reach the page.

Ideally, though, you'd just hold the work up to everything you love: in my case I should have the sense to A/B, say, the syntax of the poem against that of Borges and Cioran, the music against Bach, or John Abercrombie (an American guitarist I adore), the dynamic shape against Hitchcock or Kieslowski, and so on . . . and the formal symmetries against nature; certainly not to measure the shortfalls, you couldn't find a rule long enough – but just to keep educating those things a little. Amazing how precious all that sounded, and for no other reason than we're used to hearing poetry speak only to itself these days; and I'm as guilty as the next person for allowing it to. I'm trying to train myself out of it, though.

National Poetry Competition

The first, second and third prize-winners in the National Poetry Competition 2001 are listed below. Prizes totalled £6,500 in cash, plus publication of the winning poems in *Poetry Review*.

First Prize   *Beatrice Garland*

UNDRESSING

Like slipping stitches
or unmaking a bed
or rain from tiles,
they come tumbling off:
green dress, pale stockings,
loose silk – like mown grass
or blown roses,
subsiding in little heaps
and holding for a while
a faint perfume – soap,
warm skin – linking
these soft replicas of self.

And why stop there?
Why not like an animal,
a seed, a fruit, go on
to shed old layers of moult,
snakeskin, seed-husk, pelt
or hard green-walnut coat,
till all the roughnesses
of knocking age
are lost and something
soft, unshelled, unstained emerges blinking
into open ground?

And perhaps in time
this slow undoing will arrive
at some imagined core,
some dense and green-white bud,
weightless, untouchable.
Yes. It will come,
that last let-fall of garment,
nerve, bright hair and bone –
the rest is earth,
casements of air,
close coverings of rain,
the casual sun.

Second Prize *Ann Drysdale*

NEW FRUIT

In the last knockings of the evening sun
Eve drinks Calvados. Elsewhere in her life
She has played muse and mistress, bitch and wife.
Now all that gunpoint gamesmanship is done.
She loves the garden at this time of day.
Raising her third glass up to God, she grins;
If this is her come-uppance for her sins
It's worth a little angst along the way.
A fourth. Again the cork's slow squeaky kiss.
If, as the liquor tempts her to believe,
The Lord has one more Adam up His sleeve
He's going to have to take her as she is –
Out in the garden in a dressing-gown
Breathing old apples as the sun goes down.

Third Prize *Rhian Gallagher*

EMBRACE

Unshowered, wrestling with the sea still on our skin
when she catches me, mid-room, with a kiss.
Not a passing glance of lips, but her intended
till I press back against the wall
laughing, in a body-search pose
as ready as her to forget about dinner.
Once, in our first months, we headed down Christopher Street
starch wafting from an open laundry, the sound of a press
squeezing a line along a sleeve. We slipped
across the West Side Highway, out on the pier
pressing our faces to the fence to catch an air of sea,
distant Liberty. Winter sun pouring its heart out
over the Hudson, she stepped into me –
the cold became a memory
smudged under our winter coats.

Two guys stood on the far side of the pier
looking baffled, how long they'd been there
god knows. Gulping, knees undone, we surfaced like swimmers
and almost ran back up Christopher Street
laughing. We'd been gone an hour, the night had come
there were shelves of lights up and down the tall streets,
she was all over me. Everything had turned on.

Poet in the Gallery

JANE YEH

Masters of Colour

Royal Academy of Arts, London

IF AN ART exhibit is the visual equivalent of a literary anthology, then *Masters of Colour: Derain to Kandinsky* is a slim, eccentrically edited volume rather than a canonical survey. Focusing on the ways certain painters used colour, it mainly spans the years from 1905 to 1920, covering the Fauves in Paris, Der Blaue Reiter (the Blue Rider) in Munich, and Die Brücke (the Bridge) in Dresden and Berlin. All three groups, although influenced by Post-Impressionism, strove for modernity by painting with unprecedentedly bold, bright pigments, savage shades that broke away from realistic correspondence to the world around them – turquoise skin, magenta trees, green skies. While still depicting things like buildings and people, they were moving towards abstract art, emphasising the expressive properties of colour over faithful representation: going against nature.

Like most anthologies, the show is a hodgepodge of the boring and the brilliant. The Belgian-born Fauvist Maurice de Vlaminck surprises with his vibrant landscapes, as does Georges Braque, who, it turns out, used to compose fanciful rainbow-hued pictures before he started replicating grey Cubist exercises with Picasso. Next to them, famous names like Max Beckmann and Fernand Léger appear lacklustre. The more serious fault, however, is that the exhibit is limited to work from the Merzbacher Collection: hence no Gauguin, only one Matisse, and too many items included because the Merzbachers happen to own them (particularly the handful of sculptures, none of which involves colour). On the plus side, the show teems with variety – sorting through it is like choosing your favourites from the pic-n'-mix at Woolworths.

A sampler of late-19th-century art stars, the first gallery holds a piece each by Cézanne, Monet, Renoir, Van Gogh, Toulouse-Lautrec, and the young Picasso, fairly minor works all. (It's just as well the collection misses out Manet, whose formidable intelligence and painterly wit would have overmatched everyone in *Masters of Colour* except Vasily Kandinsky.) The rugged skull in a tiny Cézanne still-life dominates the room, although Monet's winter countryside also looks strikingly assured (a welcome change from those pastel gardens of his invariably slapped on calendars). By contrast with a typically insipid Renoir portrait – a simpering period Barbie doll – Toulouse-Lautrec's 1890 picture of a woman in a garden sings with flair, the firm, stylised lines familiar from his posters tracing her profile and hair, a cutout set against a backdrop of tangled vines. Everything is rendered in mingled streaks of green and purple – skin, dress, leaves, stalks, and shadows: so Nineties/*Yellow Book*, yet still so modern. On this evidence, at least, art historians underestimate him.

Walking into the next gallery, a long, open expanse hung largely with Fauvist paintings, is like escaping from the 19th century to the 20th – and literally a breath of fresh air after the confines of the previous chamber. Monet and company pale in comparison to the technicolour scenes on display (although brighter isn't better in the case of the Russian Constructivists also featured here). While the curators chose to plaster André Derain's banal "Boats in the Port of Collioure" across the banner out front, as well as on the show's ubiquitous posters, Vlaminck's "View from Chatou" (1906) packs more punch into its compact form than any of the sprawling Derains it faces. In the foreground, stubby brush-strokes shape a pair of trees, one on either side of the picture, flanking it like bookends; their sturdy trunks are a mélange of warm peach, orange, and carmine, roughly outlined in an inky blue. Framed in the space between them lies an azure river and a row of houses, smudgy scarlet and white blocks accented by little emerald blobs of trees. Vlaminck's rich colour contrasts make the image not merely charming, but dynamic.

Like a sandwich viewed in cross-section, his other landscape, "The Seine at Pont de Chatou" (1905–6), consists of horizontal layers stacked like bread, juxtaposing intense blues, yellows, and oranges. There's a strip of blue-and-pinkish-white sky on top, above a line of buildings which perch on the mustard yellow bank of the Seine – then a slice of water, then the nearer riverbank (also mustard), which contains horses, carriages, and indistinct people in ketchupy red and orange, shadowed with marine blue. (It's so delicious you don't even question how a horse can be so aggressively orange.)

The visual pleasure and sensuous delights of Vlaminck's work are real achievements, worth savouring in our ascetic art climate, in which conceptualism rules. For a less one-note effect, however, the exhibit offers Braque's "L'Estaque" (1906) – think David Hockney's "Mulholland Drive" series, only more sophisticated. Originally one of the Fauves, Braque creates a swashbuckling vista of curves and colours, like Gauguin after a few too many absinthes. Everything is swirling, fluid: a sinuous tree runs up the left of the canvas, with a hill sweeping down and across to the opposite corner. From this drunken perspective, a road swoops towards us in a widening curve, its bottom cut off from view by a clump of wavy strokes (tangerine, pale turquoise, lavender, chartreuse) in the foreground, presumably representing rocks. These flow into the tree's roots at left, bringing the eye full circle – dramatic composition and daring colours merged in a kind of conjuror's trick. What a shame that Braque abandoned it all for the drab rigidity of Cubism.

Even trippier than "L'Estaque", his "Landscape at La Ciotat" (1907) nearly unravels in a psychedelic dream, with an inexplicable purply-pink nimbus hovering everywhere; dizzy squiggles of Nile green, aqua, and mauve verge on pure pattern. Although Braque anchors the piece with diagonals (the sloping terrain and a meandering silhouette of distant mountains), the overall *mise en scène* is topsy-turvy, like an imaginary planet out of an Ursula LeGuin novel.

The lone portraits in the room are a Modigliani (if you've seen one, you've seen them all) and Vlaminck's arresting "Dancer at the 'Rat Mort'" (1905–6) – at first glance, just another easily palatable image of a half-naked girl, the sort that always sells well in museums (a postcard is indeed available from the gift shop). But on closer inspection, its vivid hues belie the woman's air of weariness, while her kohl-rimmed eyes stare blankly ahead and her lacquered mouth never quite smiles. Her single bared breast – its nipple matching the burnt-auburn shade of her rouged cheeks, dyed hair, and ribbon garters – seems as much a fashion accessory as her garish crimson hat (ornamented by a pink rose): external badges of femininity, or surfaces hiding the sitter's inner self. Vlaminck's brushwork calls attention to the picture's surface, too, with a heavy impasto (the pigment thick as buttercream icing) on the hat and viridescent chemise. He dabs two fierce, short strokes of rouge on the dancer's face like warpaint; similar marks dotting the yellow background imply a coarse-textured curtain. The work is a taut symphony of vicious colour, unnatural vermilions and oranges clashing with sickly greens.

In the third gallery, eight Kandinskys – admittedly the true masterpieces of the exhibit – glow like gemstones. "Lancer in Landscape" (1908) transposes the curious artificiality of medieval illuminations, with their eternal stillness, into a haunting minor key. Topiary trees tower on spindly stems, and faceless figures loom in the foreground. On a livid yellow horse, dead center amidst the murk, sits a dark rider, the mysterious lancer of the title, quietly waiting.

By the time of "Murnau – The Garden II" (1910), Kandinsky was already hurtling towards abstraction, his flowers warped almost past recognition yet burning gold against a deep sapphire ground, while a vertiginous streak of cloud and oxblood sky shoots across the upper left-hand corner. The world looks as if it's rushing away from us, the way a snapshot of a falling object comes out blurred and distorted – terrifying and exhilarating at the same time. Death? Religious ecstasy? The end of the world? If only the rest of *Masters of Colour* came so close to touching the ineffable.

Masters of Colour runs until 17 November at the Royal Academy of Arts, London; Mon-Thur, Sat 10–18.00, Fri 10–20.00 Tel: 020 7300 8000 www.royalacademy.org.uk

COURTESY OF PICSELECT

MR AND MRS MERZBACHER, THE MERZBACHER FOUNDATION AND CARAFE INVESTMENT COMPANY

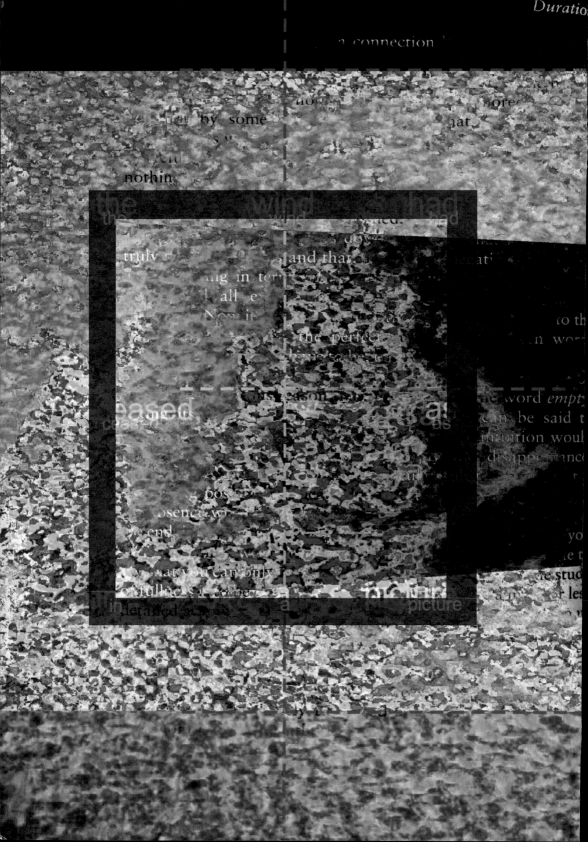

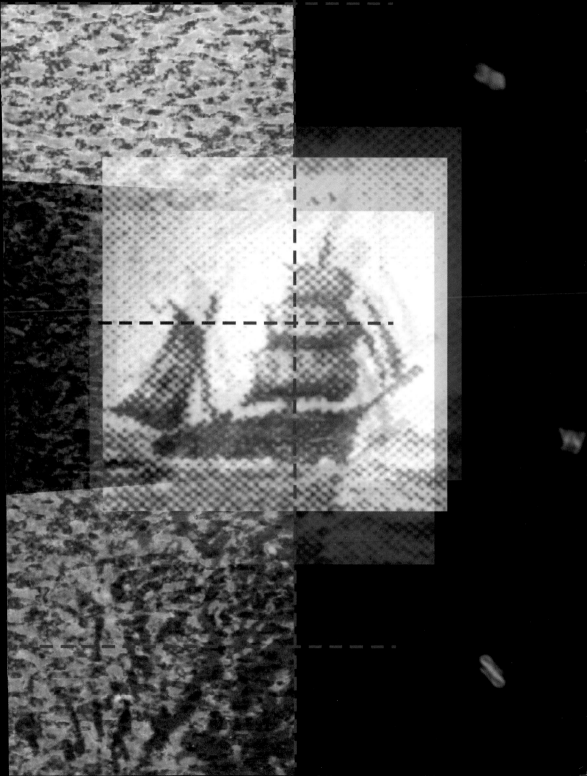

Editorial Note

First, you must catch your lobster. The silver of the lobster pots, scattered among the wild jagged rocks, is of an apparent translucence like the small old buildings with an emerald moss growing on their shoreward walls. In warm weather, out in a boat, lift the lobster-pots where they are sunk with heavy stones.

Lobsters, like crabs, are sold either live or cooked. In a glass tank supplied by a rill of cold fresh water running down a glass washboard at one end and siphoned off at the other, and so perpetually renewed, a herd of lobster is made available to the customer who may choose whichever one he wants. We inlanders, buying our needful food, pause over these slow, gigantic spiders that spin not. We pause and are bemused.

Live lobsters should be obviously alive, with clear signs of muscular activity, whether certain tentative gestures of their antennae, slow, vague wavering of the claws, or snapping of the tail. (Ask what the lobster weaves with its golden claws. The ocean knows.) Their velvet colours, mud red, bruise purple, cadaver green speckled with black, their camouflage at home, make them conspicuous in the strong day-imitating light, the incommensurable philosophers and at the same time victims herded together in the marketplace. When your lobster is lifted out of the tank to be weighed you might think of woad, of madders, of fugitive, indigo inks.

Carry home and drop into boiling water. Plop, plop. Cook those up to 750g for up to 15 minutes. Leave to cool. Lay the lobster belly-side down on a board and cut in half. Remove the stomach sac from the head. Remove the intestinal tract from the tail section. Put the lobster halves onto a baking tray and brush with melted butter. Grill under a medium high heat for 8-10 minutes. Snip off the antennae close to the head with scissors and discard.

They are peaceful, serious creatures. They know the secrets of the sea, they don't bark, and they don't gnaw upon one's monadic privacy like dogs do. Gaudy shells packed with sweet meats. Snapping and thrashing, mottled stormily.

Previous pages:
Chart (for Jorge Luis Borges and Marcel Broodthaers), by Kerry John Andrews. Kerry John Andrews is an artist, composer, and designer whose work has been exhibited internationally since 1983. As an artist and composer he works through various media, including drawing, digital media, installation, sound, and music, to explore ideas about time and the space of language and its relation to the physical world.